1 Samuel

How One Godly Man Changed A Nation

JOHN
MacARTHUR

FIRST SAMUEL
MACARTHUR BIBLE STUDIES

Copyright © 2000, John F. MacArthur, Jr. Published by W Publishing Group,
P.O. Box 141000, Nashville, TN 37214. All rights reserved. No portion of this
book may be reproduced, stored in a retrieval system, or transmitted in any form
or by any means—electronic, mechanical, photocopy, recording, or any other—
except for brief quotations in printed reviews, without the prior permission of
the publisher.

Scripture passages taken from:
The Holy Bible, *New King James Version*
Copyright © 1979, 1980, 1982 by Thomas Nelson. All rights reserved.

Cover Art by The Puckett Group.
Interior design and composition by Design Corps, Batavia, IL.

Produced with the assistance of the Livingstone Corporation. Project staff include
Dave Veerman, Christopher D. Hudson, and Amber Rae.

Project editor: Len Woods

ISBN 0-8499-5538-6

All rights reserved. *Printed in the United States of America.*

03 04 PHX 5 4

Table of Contents

FIRST SAMUEL

Introduction

First and Second Samuel were considered as one book in the earliest Hebrew manuscripts and were later divided into the two books by the translators of the Greek version of the Old Testament, the Septuagint (LXX). This division was followed by the Latin Vulgate (Vg.), English translations, and modern Hebrew Bibles. The earliest Hebrew manuscripts entitled the one book "Samuel" after the man God used to establish the kingship in Israel. Later Hebrew texts and the English versions call the divided book "1 Samuel and 2 Samuel." The LXX designated them "The First and Second Books of Kingdoms" and the Vg., "First and Second Kings," with our 1 Kings and 2 Kings entitled "Third and Fourth Kings."

Author and Date

Jewish tradition ascribed the writing of "Samuel" to Samuel himself or to Samuel, Nathan, and Gad (based on 1 Chronicles 29:29). But Samuel could not have been the writer because his death is recorded in 1 Samuel 25:1, before the events associated with David's reign had taken place. Also, Nathan and Gad were prophets of the Lord during David's lifetime and would not have been alive when the book of Samuel was written. Though the written records of these three prophets could have been used as resource material for 1 and 2 Samuel, the human author of these books is unknown. The work comes to the reader as an anonymous writing; that is, the human author speaks for the Lord and gives the divine interpretation of the events narrated.

The books of Samuel contain no clear indication of the date of their composition. That the author wrote after the division of the kingdom between Israel and Judah in 931 B.C. is clear, due to the many references to Israel and Judah as distinct entities (1 Samuel 11:8; 17:52; 18:16; 2 Samuel 5:5; 11:11; 12:8; 19:42–43; 24:1,9). Also, the statement concerning Ziklag's belonging "to the kings of Judah to this day" in 1 Samuel 27:6 gives clear evidence of a post-Solomonic date of writing. There is no such clarity concerning how late the date of writing could be; however, 1 and 2 Samuel are included in the former prophets in the Hebrew canon, along with Joshua, Judges, and 1 and 2 Kings. If the former prophets were composed as a unit, then Samuel would have been written during the Babylonian captivity (560–540 B.C.), since 2 Kings concludes during the exile (2 Kings 25:27–30). Samuel has a different literary style than Kings, however, so it was most likely penned before the Exile during the period of the divided kingdom (931–722 B.C.) and later made an integral part of the Former Prophets.

Background and Setting

The majority of the action recorded in 1 and 2 Samuel occurred in and around the central highlands in the land of Israel. The nation of Israel was largely concentrated in an area that ran about ninety miles from the hill country of Ephraim in the north (1 Samuel 1:1; 9:4) to the hill country of Judah in the south (Joshua 20:7; 21:11) and between fifteen to thirty-five miles east to west. This central spine ranges in height from 1,500 ft. to 3,300 ft. above sea level. The major cities of 1 and 2 Samuel were located in these central highlands: Shiloh, the residence of Eli and the tabernacle; Ramah, the hometown of Samuel; Gibeah, the headquarters of Saul; Bethlehem, the birthplace of David; Hebron, David's capital when he ruled over Judah; and Jerusalem, the ultimate "city of David."

The events of 1 and 2 Samuel took place between 1105 B.C., the birth of Samuel (1 Samuel 1:1–28), to 971 B.C., the last words of David (2 Samuel 23:1–7). Thus, the books span about 135 years of history. During those years, Israel was transformed from a loosely knit group of tribes under "judges" to a united nation under the reign of a centralized monarchy. The books focus primarily on Samuel (1105–1030 B.C.), Saul, who reigned from 1052 to 1011 B.C., and David, king of the united monarchy from 1011 to 971 B.C.

Historical and Theological Themes

First Samuel begins with Israel at a low point spiritually. The priesthood was corrupt (2:12–17, 22–26), the ark of the covenant was not at the tabernacle (4:3–7:2), idolatry was rampant (7:3–4), and the judges were dishonest (8:2–3). Through the influence of godly Samuel (12:23) and David (13:14), these conditions were reversed. Second Samuel concludes with the anger of the Lord being withdrawn from Israel (2 Samuel 24:25).

During the years narrated in 1 and 2 Samuel, the great empires of the ancient world were in a state of weakness. Neither Egypt nor the Mesopotamian powers, Babylon and Assyria, were threats to Israel at that time. The two nations most hostile to the Israelites were the Philistines (1 Samuel 4; 7; 13; 14; 17; 23; 31; 2 Samuel 5) to the west and the Ammonites (1 Samuel 11; 2 Samuel 10–12) to the east. The major contingent of the Philistines had migrated from the Aegean Islands and Asia Minor in the 12th century B.C. After being denied access to Egypt, they had settled among other preexisting Philistines along the Mediterranean coast of Palestine. The Philistines controlled the use of iron, which gave them a decided military and economic advantage over Israel (1 Samuel 13:19–22). The Ammonites, descendants of Lot (Genesis 19:38), lived on the Transjordan Plateau. David conquered the Philistines (2 Samuel 8:1) and the Ammonites (2 Samuel 12:29–31), along with other nations that surrounded Israel (2 Samuel 8:2–14).

First and second Samuel contain four predominant theological themes. The first is the Davidic Covenant. The books are literally framed by two references to the "anointed" king in the prayer of Hannah (1 Samuel 2:10) and the song of David (2 Samuel 22:51). These refer to the Messiah, the King who will triumph over all nations opposed to God (see Genesis 49:8–12; Numbers 24:7–9, 17–19). According to the Lord's promise, this Messiah would come through the line of David and establish David's throne forever (2 Samuel 7:12–16). The events of David's life recorded in Samuel foreshadow the actions of David's greater Son (that is, Christ) in the future.

The sovereignty of God is clearly seen in these books. For example, Samuel was born in response to Hannah's prayer (1 Samuel 9:17; 16:12–13). Also, in relation to David, it is clear that nothing could frustrate God's plan to have him rule over Israel (1 Samuel 24:20).

Third, the work of the Holy Spirit in empowering chosen individuals for divinely appointed tasks is evident. The Spirit of the Lord came upon both Saul and David after their anointing as kings (1 Samuel 10:10; 16:13), the power of the Holy Spirit brought forth prophecy (1 Samuel 10:6) and victory in battle (1 Samuel 11:6).

Fourth, the books of Samuel demonstrate the personal and national effects of sin. The sins of Eli and his sons resulted in their deaths (1 Samuel 2:12–17, 22–25; 3:10–14; 4:17–18). The lack of reverence for the ark of the covenant led to the death of a number of Israelites (1 Samuel 6:19; 2 Samuel 6:6–7). Saul's disobedience resulted in the Lord's judgment, leading to his rejection as king over Israel (1 Samuel 13:9, 13–14; 15:8–9, 20–23). Although David was forgiven for his sin of adultery and murder after his confession (2 Samuel 12:13), he still suffered the inevitable and devastating consequences of his sin (2 Samuel 12:14).

Interpretive Challenges

The books of Samuel contain a number of interpretive issues that have been widely discussed:

How did the Holy Spirit minister before Pentecost? The ministry of the Holy Spirit in 1 Samuel 10:6, 10; 16:13–14; 19:20, 23; and 2 Samuel 23:2 does not describe salvation in the New Testament sense, but an empowering by the Lord for His service (see also Judges 3:10; 6:34; 11:29; 13:25; 14:6, 19; 15:14).

What was the identity of the "distressing spirit from the Lord"? Is it a personal being, that is, a demon, or a spirit of discontent created by God in the heart (Judges 9:23)? Traditionally, this has been viewed as a demon (see note on 1 Samuel 16:14).

How did Samuel appear in 1 Samuel 28:3–5 when summoned by the medium? It seems best to understand the appearance of Samuel as the Lord allowing the dead Samuel to speak with Saul.

What is the identity of David's seed in 2 Samuel 7:12–15. Usually this is understood as Solomon; however, the New Testament applies the words to Jesus, God's Son in Hebrews 1:5 (see notes on 2 Samuel 7:12–15).

The Birth of a Leader

Opening Thought

1) What qualities make for a good leader?

Just for fun, list any ten qualities from any ten world leaders (living or dead), and create an ideal composite leader (for example, Churchill's ability to inspire; Lincoln's wisdom, etc.).

Strong Moral Compass	Judicious
Humble	Confident
Compassionate	Articulate
Charismatic	Decisive
Intelligent/Wise	Prayerful
Cautious - Conscientious	

Background of the Passage

First Samuel begins with a domestic crisis. Elkanah, of the tribe of Levi (living among the tribe of Ephraim), has two wives, Peninnah, the proud mother of numerous children, and Hannah, Elkanah's favored wife, who, in the sovereignty of God, is infertile. The situation becomes so grievous for Hannah that she prays bitterly and continuously. Ultimately she makes a vow, pledging to give back to the Lord her son, if only the Lord will graciously allow her to have one.

The Lord responds favorably to this prayer, and chapter 1 concludes with the joyous birth of this son. He is named Samuel, and true to her word, Hannah dedicates him to the Lord.

The first half of chapter 2 then contains Hannah's joyous and inspired prayer of praise, in marked contrast with her earlier prayers of desperation and anguish. The major theme is that God is a righteous judge who vindicates the humble.

These insights into the ancestry and remarkable birth of Samuel signal God's hand on Samuel's life and foreshadow the coming of a great leader. The boy will grow to be not only a great prophet in Israel (4:1), but also the last of her judges (7:17).

Bible Passage

Read 1:1—2:11, noting the key words and definitions to the right of the passage.

1 Samuel 1:1—2:11

¹ Now there was a certain man of Ramathaim Zophim, of the mountains of Ephraim, and his name [was] Elkanah the son of Jeroham, the son of Elihu, the son of Tohu, the son of Zuph, an Ephraimite.

² And he had two wives: the name of one [was] Hannah, and the name of the other Peninnah. Peninnah had children, but Hannah had no children.

³ This man went up from his city yearly to worship and sacrifice to the LORD of hosts in Shiloh. Also the two sons of Eli, Hophni and Phinehas, the priests of the LORD, [were] there.

⁴ And whenever the time came for Elkanah to make an offering, he would give portions to Peninnah his wife and to all her sons and daughters.

⁵ But to Hannah he would give a double portion, for he loved Hannah, although the LORD had closed her womb.

⁶ And her rival also provoked her severely, to make her miserable, because the LORD had closed her womb.

⁷ So it was, year by year, when she went up to the house of the LORD, that she provoked her; therefore she wept and did not eat.

⁸ Then Elkanah her husband said to her, "Hannah, why do you weep? Why do you not eat? And why is your heart grieved? [Am] I not better to you than ten sons?"

Ramathaim (v. 1)—a town about five miles north of Jerusalem, also called Ramah

two wives (v. 2)—Polygamy was never God's intention for humankind, although He tolerated it; in every biblical instance polygamy created domestic problems.

This man went up . . . yearly (v. 3)—Every year, Elkanah would attend the three mandatory feasts of Israel at the central sanctuary.

Eli (v. 3)—the High Priest at Shiloh, twenty miles north of Jerusalem; Shiloh was the site of the tabernacle and the ark of the covenant.

the Lord had closed her womb (v. 5)—Hannah's barrenness was due to God's sovereignty/providence.

her rival (v. 6)—Peninnah, Elkanah's other wife, who apparently would regularly flaunt her fertility.

9 So Hannah arose after they had finished eating and drinking in Shiloh. Now Eli the priest was sitting on the seat by the doorpost of the tabernacle of the LORD.

10 And she [was] in bitterness of soul, and prayed to the LORD and wept in anguish.

11 Then she made a vow and said, "O LORD of hosts, if You will indeed look on the affliction of Your maidservant and remember me, and not forget Your maidservant, but will give Your maidservant a male child, then I will give him to the LORD all the days of his life, and no razor shall come upon his head."

12 And it happened, as she continued praying before the LORD, that Eli watched her mouth.

13 Now Hannah spoke in her heart; only her lips moved, but her voice was not heard. Therefore Eli thought she was drunk.

14 So Eli said to her, "How long will you be drunk? Put your wine away from you!"

15 And Hannah answered and said, "No, my lord, I [am] a woman of sorrowful spirit. I have drunk neither wine nor intoxicating drink, but have poured out my soul before the LORD.

16 "Do not consider your maidservant a wicked woman, for out of the abundance of my complaint and grief I have spoken until now."

17 Then Eli answered and said, "Go in peace, and the God of Israel grant your petition which you have asked of Him."

18 And she said, "Let your maidservant find favor in your sight." So the woman went her way and ate, and her face was no longer [sad].

19 Then they rose early in the morning and worshiped before the LORD, and returned and came to their house at Ramah. And Elkanah knew Hannah his wife, and the LORD remembered her.

20 So it came to pass in the process of time that Hannah conceived and bore a son, and called his name Samuel, [saying], "Because I have asked for him from the LORD."

21 Now the man Elkanah and all his house went up to offer to the LORD the yearly sacrifice and his vow.

22 But Hannah did not go up, for she said to her

vow (v. 11)—A pledge essentially saying, "If you give me a son, I'll give him back to You that he may serve You all the days of his life"; the elements of this promise are similar to a Nazirite vow found in Numbers 6.

thought she was drunk (v. 13)—Hannah prayed inaudibly, a practice foreign to Israelites, so Eli assumed that she had been drinking.

Samuel (v. 20)—Literally this name means "name of God," but it is pronounced in such a way as to mean "heard of God" (that is, the child was an answer to her prayers).

his vow (v. 21)—Elkanah had obviously embraced Hannah's vow as his own.

weaned (v. 22)—As was customary, Samuel was probably breast-fed two to three years; then he was left in the care of Eli, the High Priest, to serve the Lord all the days of his life.

husband, "[Not] until the child is weaned; then I will take him, that he may appear before the LORD and remain there forever."

23 And Elkanah her husband said to her, "Do what seems best to you; wait until you have weaned him. Only let the LORD establish His word." So the woman stayed and nursed her son until she had weaned him.

24 Now when she had weaned him, she took him up with her, with three bulls, one ephah of flour, and a skin of wine, and brought him to the house of the LORD in Shiloh. And the child [was] young.

25 Then they slaughtered a bull, and brought the child to Eli.

26 And she said, "O my lord! As your soul lives, my lord, I [am] the woman who stood by you here, praying to the LORD.

27 "For this child I prayed, and the LORD has granted me my petition which I asked of Him.

28 "Therefore I also have lent him to the LORD; as long as he lives he shall be lent to the LORD." So they worshiped the LORD there.

1 And Hannah prayed and said: "My heart rejoices in the LORD; My horn is exalted in the LORD. I smile at my enemies, Because I rejoice in Your salvation.

2 "No one is holy like the LORD, For [there is] none besides You, Nor [is there] any rock like our God.

3 "Talk no more so very proudly; Let no arrogance come from your mouth, For the LORD [is] the God of knowledge; And by Him actions are weighed.

4 "The bows of the mighty men [are] broken, And those who stumbled are girded with strength.

5 [Those who were] full have hired themselves out for bread, And the hungry have ceased [to hunger]. Even the barren has borne seven, And she who has many children has become feeble.

6 "The LORD kills and makes alive; He brings down to the grave and brings up.

7 The LORD makes poor and makes rich; He brings low and lifts up.

8 He raises the poor from the dust [And] lifts the beggar from the ash heap, To set [them] among princes And make them inherit the throne of glory. "For the pillars of the earth [are] the

horn (2:1)—a symbol of strength and power

rock (v. 2)—a metaphor for God's strength and the security He provides for those who trust in Him

proudly . . . arrogance (v. 3)—The theme of God humbling the proud is prominent in 1 and 2 Samuel.

pillars of the earth (v. 8)—a figure of speech depicting the earth's stability in the hands of God

LORD'S, And He has set the world upon them.
9 He will guard the feet of His saints, But the
wicked shall be silent in darkness. "For by
strength no man shall prevail.
10 The adversaries of the LORD shall be broken in
pieces; From heaven He will thunder against
them. The LORD will judge the ends of the earth.
"He will give strength to His king, And exalt the
horn of His anointed."
11 Then Elkanah went to his house at Ramah. But the
child ministered to the LORD before Eli the priest.

His anointed (v. 10)—Hannah's
inspired hymn/prayer of praise
gives a prophetic glimpse into the
future when Israel will be ruled by
a victorious king who will judge
the earth righteously.

ministered to the Lord
(v. 11)—The boy Samuel assisted
Eli, the High Priest, by performing
services in and around the tabernacle complex at Shiloh.

Understanding the Text

makes him look bad, doesn't discipline Peninnah, aggravates situation by preferring Hannah, thinks he is preferable to 10 kids

2) How does the writer describe the domestic situation in the home of
Elkanah? Why are these details important to the overall message of this book?

Adversity may be overcome w/ faith

Peninnah provoked Hannah / Elkanah gave Hannah
a double portion / He loved Hannah // it extends
the motif of God bringing forth life from death

joy from obedience (Praised God even after son grew up)

3) How did Hannah's childlessness affect her? Was her response godly or not?
Why?

full of anguish + sorrow

She was ridiculed and did grieve. Bitterness in Soul?

Bargain with God in prayer, but she did follow through
Gave up burden to God when filled w/ bitterness, but
took a long time to do so ("year by year" v.7)

Prayed silently, knew God would hear

(verses to consider: Genesis 17:16–19; 25:21–26; 29:31; 30:22–24; Luke 1:5–1?)

4) What does chapter 1 say about Samuel's early childhood? Why would it be
difficult for Hannah to carry out her vow?

Samuel needed to be weaned. Eli wouldn't
be very good at it. Early childhood w/ Mom,
then separated for life of servitude. Difficult
to give up thing you want so much.

9

Cross-Reference

Compare this passage to what you have just read in chapter 1.

Judges 13:2–14

2 Now there was a certain man from Zorah, of the family of the Danites, whose name [was] Manoah; and his wife [was] barren and had no children.

3 And the Angel of the LORD appeared to the woman and said to her, "Indeed now, you are barren and have borne no children, but you shall conceive and bear a son.

4 "Now therefore, please be careful not to drink wine or [similar] drink, and not to eat anything unclean.

5 "For behold, you shall conceive and bear a son. And no razor shall come upon his head, for the child shall be a Nazirite to God from the womb; and he shall begin to deliver Israel out of the hand of the Philistines."

6 So the woman came and told her husband, saying, "A Man of God came to me, and His countenance [was] like the countenance of the Angel of God, very awesome; but I did not ask Him where He [was] from, and He did not tell me His name.

7 "And He said to me, 'Behold, you shall conceive and bear a son. Now drink no wine or [similar] drink, nor eat anything unclean, for the child shall be a Nazirite to God from the womb to the day of his death.'"

8 Then Manoah prayed to the LORD, and said, "O my Lord, please let the Man of God whom You sent come to us again and teach us what we shall do for the child who will be born."

9 And God listened to the voice of Manoah, and the Angel of God came to the woman again as she was sitting in the field; but Manoah her husband [was] not with her.

10 Then the woman ran in haste and told her husband, and said to him, "Look, the Man who came to me the [other] day has just now appeared to me!"

11 So Manoah arose and followed his wife. When he came to the Man, he said to Him, "Are You the Man who spoke to this woman?" And He said, "I [am]."

12 Manoah said, "Now let Your words come [to pass]! What will be the boy's rule of life, and his work?"

13 So the Angel of the LORD said to Manoah, "Of all that I said to the woman let her be careful.

14 "She may not eat anything that comes from the vine, nor may she drink wine or [similar] drink, nor eat anything unclean. All that I commanded her let her observe."

Exploring the Meaning

5) In what ways was the birth of Samson similar to the birth of Samuel?

Barren woman. Nazirite. Prophesied by
Angel v. Eli. Prolonged references to drinking

Faithful & prayerful parents

6) What lessons about prayer can be learned from Hannah's life?

Important to lift up burdens & also praise
God hears internal prayer

7) What words and phrases does Hannah use to describe God? How does your understanding of God fit with these biblical images?

Holy, rock, knowledge, actions are weighed,
guard, broken adversaries, thunder, judge, exalted

Summing Up . . .

"Our finite minds cannot reconcile the power of prayer with God's absolute sovereignty. As with the Trinity, and many other clearly revealed but humanly unfathomable teachings of Scripture, we simply acknowledge their absolute truth. Any seeming inconsistencies are due to the limits of our human comprehension. We know from His own Word that God is sovereign and immutable. Yet we also know from that same Word that 'the effective fervent prayer of a righteous man avails much' (James 5:16). We have our sovereign Lord's promise that 'everyone who asks, receives, and he who seeks, finds, and to him who knocks it will be opened' (Luke 11:10). Any theology that belittles the power of prayer or intensity in prayer is heresy." —_John MacArthur_

Reflecting on the Text

8) Hannah prayed fervently for a son, and God ultimately gave her a son. What seeming "impossibility" in your family needs the power of prayer this week?

Salvation, esp. for parents & Julie.

_____

_____

9) If you are a parent, how can you effectively (and practically) "dedicate" your child(ren) to the Lord? What would that look like in this century and culture?

_____

_____

_____

10) Write your own prayer of praise for something God has done in your life.

Encouraged us in happy giving & provided means to do it.

_____

Recording Your Thoughts

Ehmanois & Aiden $\xrightarrow{TX}$ CA / Bruce has insomnia
+ June Rutter

Kelly's : Boys ⟶ school
Good trip!

Oohman : Loraine - Rest

Nation

Phil + Alica - friend has cancer

_____

For further study, see the following passages:

Genesis 2:24	Exodus 7:4	Numbers 6:4–8
Numbers 24:7–9	Numbers 30:6–15	Deuteronomy 21:15–1
Deuteronomy 33:17	Joshua 5:14	Joshua 18:1
2 Samuel 1:14–16	1 Chronicles 6:27	Psalm 75:3

Out with the Old, In with the New

> ## 1 Samuel 2:12—3:21

Opening Thought

*Catholic priest molestation ....
Jim Baker
Benny Hinn*

1) Not long ago in our culture, the clergy were the most respected figures in any community. Not anymore. Widely publicized moral failures and financial scandals (especially by a few prominent tele-vangelists) have given ministers as a whole a black eye. As a result, many people have grave suspicions about the motives and actions of religious leaders.

If you were to gather a group of young ministers-in-training and had the opportunity to give them practical advice on how to rebuild the reputation of the clergy nationwide, what would you tell them?

Be an example for others at all times

Live out scriptures — be visible about it

Don't be a hypocrit

Don't value your congregation over the Lord

Background of the Passage

After detailing Samuel's birth, the writer, beginning in 2:12, gives insight into why the child was born. It is important to remember that these events took place during the period of the judges, a dark and depraved time in Israel's history. Perhaps the final verse in the book of Judges best sums up the spirit of those years: "In those days *there was* no king in Israel; everyone did *what was* right in his own eyes" (Judges 21:25).

Rather than reversing this trend and leading the nation in righteousness, Eli, the High Priest, and his sons, Hophni and Phinehas (who also served as priests), mirrored their culture and also exhibited wickedness. The sons were immoral and irreverent. The father was lax in discipline and did not forbid the young men's outrageous, rebellious behavior. Ultimately an unnamed man of God, a prophet, came and delivered a message of judgment against the house of Eli (2:27).

Meanwhile, standing out and shining brightly against this dark background of national sinfulness was the young Samuel. Having determined Eli and his sons as unfit to lead the nation spiritually, God began to speak to and through the young man. In God's wisdom and plan, Samuel would be a true prophet of God and the last judge of Israel. Such godly leadership was greatly needed then, and it is needed now.

Bible Passage

Read 2:12—3:21, noting the key words and definitions to the right of the passage.

1 Samuel 2:12—3:21

¹² *Now the sons of Eli [were] corrupt; they did not know the LORD.*

¹³ *And the priests' custom with the people [was that] when any man offered a sacrifice, the priest's servant would come with a three-pronged fleshhook in his hand while the meat was boiling.*

¹⁴ *Then he would thrust [it] into the pan, or kettle, or caldron, or pot; and the priest would take for himself all that the fleshhook brought up. So they did in Shiloh to all the Israelites who came there.*

¹⁵ *Also, before they burned the fat, the priest's servant would come and say to the man who sacrificed, "Give meat for roasting to the priest, for he will not take boiled meat from you, but raw."*

¹⁶ *And [if] the man said to him, "They should really burn the fat first; [then] you may take [as much] as your heart desires," he would then answer him, "[No], but you must give [it] now; and if not, I will take [it] by force."*

¹⁷ *Therefore the sin of the young men was very great before the LORD, for men abhorred the offering of the LORD.*

¹⁸ *But Samuel ministered before the LORD, [even as] a child, wearing a linen ephod.*

corrupt (v. 12)—Literally "sons of Belial," that is, base, worthless, and wicked; as the verse goes on to say, these religious leaders did not even have a personal experience or relationship with God.

the priests' custom (v. 13)—Worshippers were required by law to give a portion of their sacrifices to the priests; here Hophni and Phinehas took more than their share.

before they burned the fat (v. 15)—The law mandated that the fat of a sacrificial animal be burned on the altar first; in contrast Eli's sons demanded raw meat, including the fat.

But Samuel (v. 18)—Even as a young man, Samuel's behavior contrasted sharply with the disobedience of Eli's sons.

¹⁹ Moreover his mother used to make him a little robe, and bring [it] to him year by year when she came up with her husband to offer the yearly sacrifice.

²⁰ And Eli would bless Elkanah and his wife, and say, "The LORD give you descendants from this woman for the loan that was given to the LORD." Then they would go to their own home.

²¹ And the LORD visited Hannah, so that she conceived and bore three sons and two daughters. Meanwhile the child Samuel grew before the LORD.

²² Now Eli was very old; and he heard everything his sons did to all Israel, and how they lay with the women who assembled at the door of the tabernacle of meeting.

²³ So he said to them, "Why do you do such things? For I hear of your evil dealings from all the people.

²⁴ "No, my sons! For [it is] not a good report that I hear. You make the LORD's people transgress.

²⁵ "If one man sins against another, God will judge him. But if a man sins against the LORD, who will intercede for him?" Nevertheless they did not heed the voice of their father, because the LORD desired to kill them.

²⁶ And the child Samuel grew in stature, and in favor both with the LORD and men.

²⁷ Then a man of God came to Eli and said to him, "Thus says the LORD: 'Did I not clearly reveal Myself to the house of your father when they were in Egypt in Pharaoh's house?

²⁸ 'Did I not choose him out of all the tribes of Israel [to be] My priest, to offer upon My altar, to burn incense, and to wear an ephod before Me? And did I not give to the house of your father all the offerings of the children of Israel made by fire?

²⁹ 'Why do you kick at My sacrifice and My offering which I have commanded [in My] dwelling place, and honor your sons more than Me, to make yourselves fat with the best of all the offerings of Israel My people?'

³⁰ "Therefore the LORD God of Israel says: 'I said indeed [that] your house and the house of your father would walk before Me forever.' But now the LORD says: 'Far be it from Me; for those who honor Me I will honor, and those who despise Me shall be lightly esteemed.

---

the loan (v. 20)—This word is translated "granted," "asked," and "lent" in 1:27–28; it refers to Hannah's vow to God concerning her son.

lay with the women (v. 22)—Eli's sons were involved in sexual immorality with the women who served around the tabernacle; this practice was common among Israel's pagan, Canaanite neighbors.

God will judge (v. 25)—If God judges one person's sin against another, how much more will He judge blatant sins against His own holy name?

the Lord desired to kill them (v. 25)—God would kill them because they persisted in their overt, evil ways and refused ample opportunities to repent.

grew in stature, and in favor (v. 26)—In contrast to Eli's sons, Samuel was maturing spiritually and socially.

man of God (v. 27)—a prophet

why do you kick at my sacrifice . . . and honor your sons more than Me (v. 29)—By condoning (or at least allowing) the sinful behavior of his sons, Eli was demonstrating a lack of reverence for God's holy character.

But now the Lord says (v. 30)—God had promised that Aaron's descendants would always be priests, but the flagrant disobedience of the house of Eli resulted in their forfeiting the right to serve as priests.

31 'Behold, the days are coming that I will cut off your arm and the arm of your father's house, so that there will not be an old man in your house.

32 'And you will see an enemy [in My] dwelling place, [despite] all the good which God does for Israel. And there shall not be an old man in your house forever.

33 'But any of your men [whom] I do not cut off from My altar shall consume your eyes and grieve your heart. And all the descendants of your house shall die in the flower of their age.

34 'Now this [shall be] a sign to you that will come upon your two sons, on Hophni and Phinehas: in one day they shall die, both of them.

35 'Then I will raise up for Myself a faithful priest [who] shall do according to what [is] in My heart and in My mind. I will build him a sure house, and he shall walk before My anointed forever.

36 'And it shall come to pass that everyone who is left in your house will come [and] bow down to him for a piece of silver and a morsel of bread, and say, "Please, put me in one of the priestly positions, that I may eat a piece of bread."'"

1 Then the boy Samuel ministered to the LORD before Eli. And the word of the LORD was rare in those days; [there was] no widespread revelation.

2 And it came to pass at that time, while Eli [was] lying down in his place, and when his eyes had begun to grow so dim that he could not see,

3 and before the lamp of God went out in the tabernacle of the LORD where the ark of God [was], and while Samuel was lying down,

4 that the LORD called Samuel. And he answered, "Here I am!"

5 So he ran to Eli and said, "Here I am, for you called me." And he said, "I did not call; lie down again." And he went and lay down.

6 Then the LORD called yet again, "Samuel!" So Samuel arose and went to Eli, and said, "Here I am, for you called me." He answered, "I did not call, my son; lie down again."

7 (Now Samuel did not yet know the LORD, nor was the word of the LORD yet revealed to him.)

8 And the LORD called Samuel again the third time. Then he arose and went to Eli, and said, "Here I

---

will not be an old man in your house (v. 31)—God's judgment would cut short the lives of Eli's descendants.

a sign to you (v. 34)—The deaths of Hophni and Phinehas on the same day would serve to confirm the prophecy.

I will raise up for Myself a faithful priest (v. 35)—fulfilled in the accession of Zadok and his family to the priestly office during the time of Solomon

My anointed (v. 35)—A reference to the Messiah who will defeat God's enemies and rule in the Millennium.

the boy Samuel (3:1)—probably a teenager by this time

the word of the Lord was rare (v. 1)—Prophetic activity was extremely limited during the time of the judges; perhaps the idea is that because few were obeying God's Word, God stopped speaking.

Samuel did not yet know the Lord (v. 7)—Samuel had not yet encountered the Lord in a personal way, nor had he received any kind of prophetic revelation.

Then Eli perceived (v. 8)—This indicates the High Priest's spiritual dullness; he should have discerned what was happening long before he finally did.

am, for you did call me." Then Eli perceived that the LORD had called the boy.

9 *Therefore Eli said to Samuel, "Go, lie down; and it shall be, if He calls you, that you must say, 'Speak, LORD, for Your servant hears.'" So Samuel went and lay down in his place.*

10 *Now the LORD came and stood and called as at other times, "Samuel! Samuel!" And Samuel answered, "Speak, for Your servant hears."*

11 *Then the LORD said to Samuel: "Behold, I will do something in Israel at which both ears of everyone who hears it will tingle.*

12 *"In that day I will perform against Eli all that I have spoken concerning his house, from beginning to end.*

13 *"For I have told him that I will judge his house forever for the iniquity which he knows, because his sons made themselves vile, and he did not restrain them.*

14 *"And therefore I have sworn to the house of Eli that the iniquity of Eli's house shall not be atoned for by sacrifice or offering forever."*

15 *So Samuel lay down until morning, and opened the doors of the house of the LORD. And Samuel was afraid to tell Eli the vision.*

16 *Then Eli called Samuel and said, "Samuel, my son!" And he answered, "Here I am."*

17 *And he said, "What [is] the word that [the LORD] spoke to you? Please do not hide [it] from me. God do so to you, and more also, if you hide anything from me of all the things that He said to you."*

18 *Then Samuel told him everything, and hid nothing from him. And he said, "It [is] the LORD. Let Him do what seems good to Him."*

19 *So Samuel grew, and the LORD was with him and let none of his words fall to the ground.*

20 *And all Israel from Dan to Beersheba knew that Samuel [had been] established as a prophet of the LORD.*

21 *Then the LORD appeared again in Shiloh. For the LORD revealed Himself to Samuel in Shiloh by the word of the LORD.*

hears (v. 10)—listens with a view toward obeying

ears . . . will tingle (v. 11)—a message of impending destruction on Eli's house

did not restrain them (v. 13)—Eli was held accountable by God for not judging his own sinful sons.

shall not be atoned (v. 14)—For their defiant, presumptuous sin there would be no atonement.

God do so to you, and more also (v. 17)—In this imprecatory oath, Eli called on God to punish Samuel if he did not reveal all that he knew.

Let Him do what seems good (v. 18)—Eli resigned himself to the sovereign will and purpose of God.

let none of his words fall to the ground (v. 19)—God fulfilled all that Samuel had said, authenticating Samuel's status as a prophet.

See v. 20 → how Hannah got more kids

Understanding the Text

2) In what specific ways were the sons of Eli sinning against the Lord? How did God eventually confront this behavior?

lay w/ women, took more than share of sacrifice, didn't burn fat

3) How is Samuel described in contrast to the sons of Eli?

Samuel ministered before God, held favor w/ God

4) What happened in Samuel's first encounter with the Lord?

Did not know who was calling, received prophecy

Cross-Reference

Compare this passage concerning the call of Jeremiah to what you have just read about God's call of Samuel in chapter 3.

Jeremiah 1:4–10

⁴ *Then the word of the LORD came to me, saying:*

⁵ *"Before I formed you in the womb I knew you; Before you were born I sanctified you; I ordained you a prophet to the nations."*

⁶ *Then said I: "Ah, Lord GOD! Behold, I cannot speak, for I [am] a youth."*

⁷ *But the LORD said to me: "Do not say, 'I [am] a youth,' For you shall go to all to whom I send you, And whatever I command you, you shall speak.*

⁸ *Do not be afraid of their faces, For I [am] with you to deliver you," says the LORD.*

⁹ *Then the LORD put forth His hand and touched my mouth, and the LORD said to me: "Behold, I have put My words in your mouth.*

¹⁰ *See, I have this day set you over the nations and over the kingdoms, To root out and to pull down, To destroy and to throw down, To build and to plant."*

Exploring the Meaning

5) Like Samuel, Jeremiah was called at an early age. What do both of these passages reveal about "the call of God"? About God's nature?

_____

_____

6) How could a godly young man like Samuel grow up in a wicked household like Eli's? What challenges would he face?

Eli seemed a good teacher, but not
a good example. Samuel faced temptation

_____

7) What does God's severe judgment of His own priests mean for Christians today who persist in sin?

Nothing good

_____

Summing Up . . .

"If you have met with the frowns of providence, perhaps some way of sin in your life explains why. When you have received sore rebukes and chastisements, it is very probable that you're practicing a sinful habit or tolerating an evil act is what has caused you the trouble. Sometimes God is exceedingly severe in His dealings with His own people for their sins in this world. . . .

"How harshly did God deal with Eli for living in the sin of not restraining his children from wickedness! Both sons were killed in one day, and Eli himself died a violent death. The ark was taken into captivity (chapter 4). Eli's house was cursed forever; God Himself swore that the iniquity in Eli's house would never be purged by sacrifice and offerings (3:13–14). The priesthood was taken from Eli and given to another line. And there never again was an old man in Eli's family (2:31). Is the way of sin in which you live the reason for the rebukes of providence you have met with?" —_John MacArthur_

Reflecting on the Text

8) According to 1 Peter 2:9, Christians are a New Testament "priesthood." What are the implications of this fact if we live in sin and defiance as the Old Testament priests Hophni and Phinehas did?

We are "corrupt", we "kick at this sacrifice & offering."

9) Samuel was extremely sensitive to what God was saying to Him. What are some things *you* can do specifically and practically this week to be more in tune with God's leading?

Listen

10) List five religious leaders for whom you will commit to pray this week—that they might live and minister to the glory of God.

Corey, Leslie, Frank, Pope

Recording Your Thoughts

Chicken Pie!   _Politics_

Ehmanns

Adlai - job

Pastor Appreciation

For further study, see the following passages:

Exodus 27:10, 21	Exodus 28:6–14, 31	Exodus 30:8
Exodus 38:8	Leviticus 2:3, 10	Leviticus 7:31
Leviticus 24:11–23	Numbers 25:13, 18–19	Deuteronomy 18:3, 21–22
1 Kings 1:7–8	Jeremiah 19:3	1 Corinthians 6:15
Luke 2:52		

The Judgeship of Samuel

Opening Thought

1) It's often said: "Desperate times call for desperate measures." When did you face "desperate times"? What "desperate measures" did you take?

bar exam — prayed, vented, studied

2) Imagine that through a wild sequence of events, you were named "benevolent dictator" of the entire country. What ten actions would you implement in order to turn the nation around?

Give everyone perfect understanding of & faith in salvation

Background of the Passage

After repeating the same depressing cycle—sin, servitude, supplication, salvation—seven times over a period of almost five hundred years (the time of the judges), Israel was in terrible condition. Many reasons could be cited, but one stands out: The decadent nation was led by corrupt spiritual leaders.

Yet, according to the first chapters of 1 Samuel, even in the midst of this mess, God was working and in control. Behind the scenes, and in contrast to the times, God was preparing a godly young man named Samuel to provide a new kind of leadership for His covenant people. Samuel would serve not only as the last of the judges, but also as a prophet, speaking God's truth to a nation wallowing in sin.

In chapters 4—7, the judgment of God comes, as prophesied, to Eli's house at the hands of the wicked Philistines. In that same attack, the Ark of the Covenant is captured and taken to Ashdod, whereupon its presence results in punishment for its Philistine captors.

Following the return of the Ark, Samuel leads Israel in a time of national repentance. At long last there is peace in the land.

Bible Passage

Read 4:1—7:17, noting the key words and definitions to the right of the passage.

1 Samuel 4:1—7:17

¹ *And the word of Samuel came to all Israel. Now Israel went out to battle against the Philistines, and encamped beside Ebenezer; and the Philistines encamped in Aphek.*

² *Then the Philistines put themselves in battle array against Israel. And when they joined battle, Israel was defeated by the Philistines, who killed about four thousand men of the army in the field.*

³ *And when the people had come into the camp, the elders of Israel said, "Why has the LORD defeated us today before the Philistines? Let us bring the ark of the covenant of the LORD from Shiloh to us, that when it comes among us it may save us from the hand of our enemies."*

⁴ *So the people sent to Shiloh, that they might bring from there the ark of the covenant of the LORD of hosts, who dwells [between] the cherubim. And the two sons of Eli, Hophni, and Phinehas, [were] there with the ark of the covenant of God.*

⁵ *And when the ark of the covenant of the LORD came into the camp, all Israel shouted so loudly that the earth shook.*

⁶ *Now when the Philistines heard the noise of the shout, they said, "What [does] the sound of this great shout in the camp of the Hebrews [mean]?" Then they understood that the ark of the LORD had come into the camp.*

⁷ *So the Philistines were afraid, for they said, "God has come into the camp!" And they said, "Woe to us! For such a thing has never happened before.*

⁸ *"Woe to us! Who will deliver us from the hand of these mighty gods? These [are] the gods who struck the Egyptians with all the plagues in the wilderness.*

Philistines (v. 1)—Non-Semitic peoples who lived along the coast of southern Canaan and were an ever present enemy to Israel from the period of the judges through the end of King David's reign.

Ebenezer (v. 1)—"stone of help"

Why has the Lord defeated us? (v. 3)—Because the Lord fought their battles (2:10), defeat meant that He had not been present.

Let us bring the ark (v. 3)—This symbol of the presence of God was wrongly viewed as a kind of good luck charm by the Israelites.

Hebrews (v. 6)—This name had been applied to Abram and his descendants.

the gods who struck the Egyptian (v. 8)—Though their theology was wrong, the Philistines had heard of the miraculous exodus from Egypt.

9 "Be strong and conduct yourselves like men, you Philistines, that you do not become servants of the Hebrews, as they have been to you. Conduct yourselves like men, and fight!"

10 So the Philistines fought, and Israel was defeated, and every man fled to his tent. There was a very great slaughter, and there fell of Israel thirty thousand foot soldiers.

11 Also the ark of God was captured; and the two sons of Eli, Hophni and Phinehas, died.

12 Then a man of Benjamin ran from the battle line the same day, and came to Shiloh with his clothes torn and dirt on his head.

13 Now when he came, there was Eli, sitting on a seat by the wayside watching, for his heart trembled for the ark of God. And when the man came into the city and told [it], all the city cried out.

14 When Eli heard the noise of the outcry, he said, "What [does] the sound of this tumult [mean]?" And the man came quickly and told Eli.

15 Eli was ninety-eight years old, and his eyes were so dim that he could not see.

16 Then the man said to Eli, "I [am] he who came from the battle. And I fled today from the battle line." And he said, "What happened, my son?"

17 So the messenger answered and said, "Israel has fled before the Philistines, and there has been a great slaughter among the people. Also your two sons, Hophni and Phinehas, are dead; and the ark of God has been captured."

18 Then it happened, when he made mention of the ark of God, that Eli fell off the seat backward by the side of the gate; and his neck was broken and he died, for the man was old and heavy. And he had judged Israel forty years.

19 Now his daughter-in-law, Phinehas' wife, was with child, [due] to be delivered; and when she heard the news that the ark of God was captured, and that her father-in-law and her husband were dead, she bowed herself and gave birth, for her labor pains came upon her.

20 And about the time of her death the women who stood by her said to her, "Do not fear, for you have borne a son." But she did not answer, nor did she regard [it].

21 Then she named the child Ichabod, saying, "The glory has departed from Israel!" because the ark of God had been captured and because of her father-in-law and her husband.

22 And she said, "The glory has departed from Israel, for the ark of God has been captured."

clothes torn and dirt on his head (v. 12)—a recognized sign of mourning over national calamity

Ichabod (v. 21)—Means "Where is the glory?" or "no glory"; and was given to memorialize the loss of the ark, the symbol of God's presence among His people

¹ Then the Philistines took the ark of God and brought it from Ebenezer to Ashdod.

² When the Philistines took the ark of God, they brought it into the temple of Dagon and set it by Dagon.

³ And when the people of Ashdod arose early in the morning, there was Dagon, fallen on its face to the earth before the ark of the LORD. So they took Dagon and set it in its place again.

⁴ And when they arose early the next morning, there was Dagon, fallen on its face to the ground before the ark of the LORD. The head of Dagon and both the palms of its hands [were] broken off on the threshold; only Dagon's torso was left of it.

⁵ Therefore neither the priests of Dagon nor any who come into Dagon's house tread on the threshold of Dagon in Ashdod to this day.

⁶ But the hand of the LORD was heavy on the people of Ashdod, and He ravaged them and struck them with tumors, [both] Ashdod and its territory.

⁷ And when the men of Ashdod saw how [it was], they said, "The ark of the God of Israel must not remain with us, for His hand is harsh toward us and Dagon our god."

⁸ Therefore they sent and gathered to themselves all the lords of the Philistines, and said, "What shall we do with the ark of the God of Israel?" And they answered, "Let the ark of the God of Israel be carried away to Gath." So they carried the ark of the God of Israel away.

⁹ So it was, after they had carried it away, that the hand of the LORD was against the city with a very great destruction; and He struck the men of the city, both small and great, and tumors broke out on them.

¹⁰ Therefore they sent the ark of God to Ekron. So it was, as the ark of God came to Ekron, that the Ekronites cried out, saying, "They have brought the ark of the God of Israel to us, to kill us and our people!"

¹¹ So they sent and gathered together all the lords of the Philistines, and said, "Send away the ark of the God of Israel, and let it go back to its own place, so that it does not kill us and our people." For there was a deadly destruction throughout all the city; the hand of God was very heavy there.

¹² And the men who did not die were stricken with the tumors, and the cry of the city went up to heaven.

¹ Now the ark of the LORD was in the country of the Philistines seven months.

Ashdod (5:1)—one of the five principal Philistine cities, located about thirty-three miles west of Jerusalem

Dagon (v. 2)—Perhaps the most prominent deity of the polytheistic Philistines, Dagon was the god of vegetation or grain; placing the ark in Dagon's temple was intended to picture Dagon's superiority.

head . . . hands broken off (v. 4)—God's judgment on this false idol

tumors (v. 6)—probably boils or sores caused by an epidemic similar to bubonic plague

² And the Philistines called for the priests and the diviners, saying, "What shall we do with the ark of the LORD? Tell us how we should send it to its place."

³ So they said, "If you send away the ark of the God of Israel, do not send it empty; but by all means return [it] to Him [with] a trespass offering. Then you will be healed, and it will be known to you why His hand is not removed from you."

⁴ Then they said, "What [is] the trespass offering which we shall return to Him?" They answered, "Five golden tumors and five golden rats, [according to] the number of the lords of the Philistines. For the same plague [was] on all of you and on your lords.

⁵ "Therefore you shall make images of your tumors and images of your rats that ravage the land, and you shall give glory to the God of Israel; perhaps He will lighten His hand from you, from your gods, and from your land.

⁶ "Why then do you harden your hearts as the Egyptians and Pharaoh hardened their hearts? When He did mighty things among them, did they not let the people go, that they might depart?

⁷ "Now therefore, make a new cart, take two milk cows which have never been yoked, and hitch the cows to the cart; and take their calves home, away from them.

⁸ "Then take the ark of the LORD and set it on the cart; and put the articles of gold which you are returning to Him [as] a trespass offering in a chest by its side. Then send it away, and let it go.

⁹ "And watch: if it goes up the road to its own territory, to Beth Shemesh, [then] He has done us this great evil. But if not, then we shall know that [it is] not His hand [that] struck us—it happened to us by chance."

¹⁰ Then the men did so; they took two milk cows and hitched them to the cart, and shut up their calves at home.

¹¹ And they set the ark of the LORD on the cart, and the chest with the gold rats and the images of their tumors.

¹² Then the cows headed straight for the road to Beth Shemesh, [and] went along the highway, lowing as they went, and did not turn aside to the right hand or the left. And the lords of the Philistines went after them to the border of Beth Shemesh.

¹³ Now [the people of] Beth Shemesh [were] reaping their wheat harvest in the valley; and they lifted their eyes and saw the ark, and rejoiced to see [it].

the priests and the diviners (6:2)—pagan religious authorities summoned to attempt to find out how to appease God so that He would stop the plague

trespass offering (v. 3)—an acknowledgment and compensation for dishonoring the God of Israel

Five golden tumors and five golden rats (v. 4)—a primitive way for the Philistines to demonstrate to God that they understood why He was angry

give glory to the God of Israel (v. 5)—acknowledging their sin and God's supremacy

never been yoked (v. 7)—This test would demonstrate conclusively whether God was behind this calamity; untrained cows would not pull a cart (and certainly would not leave their calves) unless God were directing them.

¹⁴ Then the cart came into the field of Joshua of Beth Shemesh, and stood there; a large stone [was] there. So they split the wood of the cart and offered the cows as a burnt offering to the LORD.

¹⁵ The Levites took down the ark of the LORD and the chest that [was] with it, in which [were] the articles of gold, and put [them] on the large stone. Then the men of Beth Shemesh offered burnt offerings and made sacrifices the same day to the LORD.

¹⁶ So when the five lords of the Philistines had seen [it], they returned to Ekron the same day.

¹⁷ These [are] the golden tumors which the Philistines returned [as] a trespass offering to the LORD: one for Ashdod, one for Gaza, one for Ashkelon, one for Gath, one for Ekron;

¹⁸ and the golden rats, [according to] the number of all the cities of the Philistines [belonging] to the five lords, [both] fortified cities and country villages, even as far as the large [stone of] Abel on which they set the ark of the LORD, [which stone remains] to this day in the field of Joshua of Beth Shemesh.

¹⁹ Then He struck the men of Beth Shemesh, because they had looked into the ark of the LORD. He struck fifty thousand and seventy men of the people, and the people lamented because the LORD had struck the people with a great slaughter.

²⁰ And the men of Beth Shemesh said, "Who is able to stand before this holy LORD God? And to whom shall it go up from us?"

²¹ So they sent messengers to the inhabitants of Kirjath Jearim, saying, "The Philistines have brought back the ark of the LORD; come down [and] take it up with you."

¹ Then the men of Kirjath Jearim came and took the ark of the LORD, and brought it into the house of Abinadab on the hill, and consecrated Eleazar his son to keep the ark of the LORD.

² So it was that the ark remained in Kirjath Jearim a long time; it was there twenty years. And all the house of Israel lamented after the LORD.

³ Then Samuel spoke to all the house of Israel, saying, "If you return to the LORD with all your hearts, [then] put away the foreign gods and the Ashtoreths from among you, and prepare your hearts for the LORD, and serve Him only; and He will deliver you from the hand of the Philistines."

⁴ So the children of Israel put away the Baals and the Ashtoreths, and served the LORD only.

burnt offering (v. 14)—Because the cows had been used for sacred purposes, they could not be used for everyday purposes; thus the men of Beth Shemesh sacrificed them.

looked into the ark (v. 19)—a sin of presumption and irreverence, resulting in fierce judgment

prepare your hearts for the Lord (7:3)—a reminder of the repeated cycle in the book of Judges (apostasy, oppression, repentance, and deliverance) and a preview of chapter 7

the Baals and the Ashtoreths (v. 4)—Canaanite fertility gods that the Israelites had sinfully begun to worship

5 And Samuel said, "Gather all Israel to Mizpah, and I will pray to the LORD for you."
6 So they gathered together at Mizpah, drew water, and poured [it] out before the LORD. And they fasted that day, and said there, "We have sinned against the LORD." And Samuel judged the children of Israel at Mizpah.
7 Now when the Philistines heard that the children of Israel had gathered together at Mizpah, the lords of the Philistines went up against Israel. And when the children of Israel heard [of it], they were afraid of the Philistines.
8 So the children of Israel said to Samuel, "Do not cease to cry out to the LORD our God for us, that He may save us from the hand of the Philistines."
9 And Samuel took a suckling lamb and offered [it as] a whole burnt offering to the LORD. Then Samuel cried out to the LORD for Israel, and the LORD answered him.
10 Now as Samuel was offering up the burnt offering, the Philistines drew near to battle against Israel. But the LORD thundered with a loud thunder upon the Philistines that day, and so confused them that they were overcome before Israel.
11 And the men of Israel went out of Mizpah and pursued the Philistines, and drove them back as far as below Beth Car.
12 Then Samuel took a stone and set [it] up between Mizpah and Shen, and called its name Ebenezer, saying, "Thus far the LORD has helped us."
13 So the Philistines were subdued, and they did not come anymore into the territory of Israel. And the hand of the LORD was against the Philistines all the days of Samuel.
14 Then the cities which the Philistines had taken from Israel were restored to Israel, from Ekron to Gath; and Israel recovered its territory from the hands of the Philistines. Also there was peace between Israel and the Amorites.
15 And Samuel judged Israel all the days of his life.
16 He went from year to year on a circuit to Bethel, Gilgal, and Mizpah, and judged Israel in all those places.
17 But he always returned to Ramah, for his home [was] there. There he judged Israel, and there he built an altar to the LORD.

drew water, and poured it out before the Lord (v. 6)—a symbol of repentance

Samuel judged (v. 6)—Samuel assumed Eli's role, providing domestic and military leadership for Israel.

the Lord thundered (v. 10)—a fulfillment of Hannah's prayer (2:10)

Thus far the Lord has helped us (v. 12)—a recognition of God's sovereignty and faithfulness

a circuit (v. 16)—an annual trip so as to manage the affairs of the people

Understanding the Text

3) What did the Israelites think would happen as they prepared to go out and battle the Philistines? Were they right or wrong? Why?

Thought they would win ; wrong ; God forsaken as they had forsaken God

4) What happened when the Philistines captured the Ark of the Covenant, and what did these events demonstrate?

Dissed Dagon — One God sovereign

5) In what ways was Samuel different than his predecessor, Eli?

Called on people to forsake idols / gods

Cross-Reference

Compare God's dealings with "the children of Israel" to what Hebrews says.

Hebrews 12:5–11

⁵ *And you have forgotten the exhortation which speaks to you as to sons: "My son, do not despise the chastening of the Lord, Nor be discouraged when you are rebuked by Him;*

⁶ *For whom the Lord loves He chastens, And scourges every son whom He receives."*

⁷ *If you endure chastening, God deals with you as with sons; for what son is there whom a father does not chasten?*

⁸ *But if you are without chastening, of which all have become partakers, then you are illegitimate and not sons.*

⁹ *Furthermore, we have had human fathers who corrected [us], and we paid [them] respect. Shall we not much more readily be in subjection to the Father of spirits and live?*

¹⁰ *For they indeed for a few days chastened [us] as seemed [best] to them, but He for [our] profit, that [we] may be partakers of His holiness.*

¹¹ *Now no chastening seems to be joyful for the present, but painful; nevertheless, afterward it yields the peaceable fruit of righteousness to those who have been trained by it.*

Exploring the Meaning

6) How does this New Testament passage underscore what we see taking place in chapters 4—7? Are the people of God exempt from God's displeasure over sin?

People of God esp. subject to discipline

7) The Philistines worshiped the god Dagon; the Israelites are said to have worshiped the Baals and the Astoreths. What does the passage teach about the consequences of idolatry? Why does it elicit such a strong response from God?

First Commandment

8) What specific steps were involved in Israel's repentance?

Sacrifices, rejection of idols/gods, renewal of faith

Summing Up . . .

"Lest we think that contemporary, sophisticated man has risen above such crude foolishness [as idolatry], we have only to consider the monumental increase in astrology and other occultic practices during the last few decades. . . . Many leading world figures, including noted scientists, are said to consult their horoscopes or occult advisers for information from star movement or tea leaves before making major decisions or taking extended trips.

"There have always been people who worship the idols of wealth, health, pleasure, prestige, sex, sports, education, entertainment, celebrities, success, and power. At no time in history have those forms of idolatry been more pervasive and corrupting than in our own day." —*John MacArthur*

Reflecting on the Text

9) The ancient Hebrews were superstitious regarding the Ark of the Covenant. Instead of seeing it as a symbol, they foolishly viewed it as a magical object. What religious symbols (that is, a cross, a Bible, a church building, etc.) might you be tempted to regard in this primitive way?

_____

_____

10) As you think about your life, in what areas do you tend to resist the Lordship of Christ? What does this chapter reveal about God's dealings with those who stubbornly cling to sin? What desperate measures do you need to take?

_____

_____

11) In what specific ways can you be a Samuel in your family, church, or community this week? That is, what would spiritual and moral leadership look like in your life?

_____Be more open_____

_____

Recording Your Thoughts

praise - Aiden   prayer - in-law visit   Ehmann.

Andrew   Julie   moving

Rudders (missionaries Vietnam)   Jennifer

For further study, see the following passages:

Genesis 10:14	Exodus 7:14	Exodus 8:15
Numbers 4:20	Numbers 14:42	Judges 1:28
Judges 16:23	2 Samuel 4:12	2 Samuel 6:2, 6–7
2 Samuel 15:32	2 Samuel 23:16	1 Chronicles 13:6

Israel Demands a King!

1 Samuel 8:1–22

Opening Thought

1) It is common for adults to lecture children and youth about the dangers of peer pressure. This phenomenon causes one to feel an inordinate desire to fit in and to be like everyone else in actions, dress, behavior, and so forth.

How much peer pressure do adults feel? Give specific examples of ways adults try to "keep up with the Joneses." With which of these temptations do you most struggle?

_____

_____

_____

Background of the Passage

Until the time of Samuel, Israel had suffered about five hundred continuous years of political turmoil and military failure, not to mention a roller-coaster-like spiritual experience. Historians agree that the time of the judges was one of the darkest periods in Israel's existence.

Replacing the spiritually anemic Eli (and his evil sons Hophni and Phinehas), the prophet/judge Samuel had, with God's help, restored some semblance of stability and morality to the nation. For a change, Israel's future looked bright and hopeful. As Samuel aged, however, old cycles began to reappear.

Samuel's plan was to groom his sons to take his place. Ironically, however, just as with the house of Eli before him, Samuel's sons were unfit to lead. Despite their godly heritage, they took bribes and perverted justice.

So the elders of the tribes of Israel approached Samuel with the request for a king. As chapter 8 indicates, this request was rooted in a sinful desire to be like all the other nations. In essence by caving in to a kind of international peer pressure, the people of Israel were rejecting God. Not surprisingly, things got much worse in Israel before they got better.

Bible Passage

Read 8:1–22, noting the key words and definitions to the right of the passage.

1 Samuel 8:1–22

¹ *Now it came to pass when Samuel was old that he made his sons judges over Israel.*

² *The name of his firstborn was Joel, and the name of his second, Abijah; [they were] judges in Beersheba.*

³ *But his sons did not walk in his ways; they turned aside after dishonest gain, took bribes, and perverted justice.*

⁴ *Then all the elders of Israel gathered together and came to Samuel at Ramah,*

⁵ *and said to him, "Look, you are old, and your sons do not walk in your ways. Now make us a king to judge us like all the nations."*

⁶ *But the thing displeased Samuel when they said, "Give us a king to judge us." So Samuel prayed to the LORD.*

⁷ *And the LORD said to Samuel, "Heed the voice of the people in all that they say to you; for they have not rejected you, but they have rejected Me, that I should not reign over them.*

⁸ *"According to all the works which they have done since the day that I brought them up out of Egypt, even to this day—with which they have forsaken Me and served other gods—so they are doing to you also.*

⁹ *"Now therefore, heed their voice. However, you shall solemnly forewarn them, and show them the behavior of the king who will reign over them."*

¹⁰ *So Samuel told all the words of the LORD to the people who asked him for a king.*

¹¹ *And he said, "This will be the behavior of the king who will reign over you: He will take your*

Samuel was old (v. 1)—probably about sixty years old (1043 B.C.)

his sons did not walk in his ways (v. 3)—Samuel's sons' desire for riches led them to take bribes and thereby pervert justice.

Now make us a king . . . like all the nations (v. 5)—similar to the Canaanite city-states that filled the land when Joshua led the people of Israel into the Promised Land, and similar to their neighbors during the time of the judges

Heed the voice of the people (v. 7)—This request did not surprise God; in fact, He had spoken previously about future kings in Israel.

they have . . . rejected . . . Me (v. 7)—This petition constituted a desire for a visible human ruler rather than God's reign over the nation.

you shall solemnly forewarn them (v. 9)—God instructed Samuel to describe in great detail the burdens of a monarchy: a military draft, taxes, governmental seizure of property and citizenry, and limits on freedom.

sons and appoint [them] for his own chariots and [to be] his horsemen, and [some] will run before his chariots.

12 "He will appoint captains over his thousands and captains over his fifties, [will set some] to plow his ground and reap his harvest, and [some] to make his weapons of war and equipment for his chariots.

13 "He will take your daughters [to be] perfumers, cooks, and bakers.

14 "And he will take the best of your fields, your vineyards, and your olive groves, and give [them] to his servants.

15 "He will take a tenth of your grain and your vintage, and give it to his officers and servants.

16 "And he will take your male servants, your female servants, your finest young men, and your donkeys, and put [them] to his work.

17 "He will take a tenth of your sheep. And you will be his servants.

18 "And you will cry out in that day because of your king whom you have chosen for yourselves, and the LORD will not hear you in that day."

19 Nevertheless the people refused to obey the voice of Samuel; and they said, "No, but we will have a king over us,

20 that we also may be like all the nations, and that our king may judge us and go out before us and fight our battles."

21 And Samuel heard all the words of the people, and he repeated them in the hearing of the LORD.

22 So the LORD said to Samuel, "Heed their voice, and make them a king." And Samuel said to the men of Israel, "Every man go to his city."

you will cry out . . . because of your king (v. 18)—The people would live to regret this decision.

the Lord will not hear you (v. 18)—God pledged not to deliver the people from the eventual oppression they would experience from their human monarch.

Nevertheless. . . . "we will have a king over us" (v. 19)— The people stubbornly refused to listen to Samuel's dire warning.

fight our battles (v. 20)—an overt rejection of the invisible God of Israel as their protector and warrior and an explicit desire for a visible king (like all the surrounding nations had) who could and would lead them in battle

Understanding the Text

2) What happened when Samuel attempted to make his sons judges over Israel? Why were they unfit to serve in this capacity?

_____

_____

_____

3) What was Samuel's response when the people came to him and demanded a king? What specific warnings did he give the people?

_____

_____

_____

4) What reasons are cited for the people's refusal to listen to Samuel?

_____

_____

_____

Cross-Reference

Compare this New Testament passage with the message of chapter 8.

1 Peter 2:9–12
⁹ *But you [are] a chosen generation, a royal priesthood, a holy nation, His own special people, that you may proclaim the praises of Him who called you out of darkness into His marvelous light;*
¹⁰ *who once [were] not a people but [are] now the people of God, who had not obtained mercy but now have obtained mercy.*
¹¹ *Beloved, I beg [you] as sojourners and pilgrims, abstain from fleshly lusts which war against the soul,*
¹² *having your conduct honorable among the Gentiles, that when they speak against you as evildoers, they may, by [your] good works which they observe, glorify God in the day of visitation.*

Exploring the Meaning

5) What reasons does this passage give for the people of God to be different from the people of the world?

_____

_____

_____

6) Read Romans 12:1–2. What is the solution for believers who live in a world that attempts to conform them to its pattern of thinking and living? What does that mean?

_____

_____

7) How is it that a godly man like Samuel could rear such wayward sons? And what about the converse situation seen often in the Bible: How is that godly children can come from ungodly parentage?

_____

_____

Summing Up . . .

"Many believers are inclined to accommodate to nearly every worldly practice. Under the pretense of relevance, they copy the world's materialistic and immoral ways. When the world becomes preoccupied with material things, so has the church. When the world lowers its sexual standards, so has the church. When the world becomes entertainment crazed, so has the church. When the world glorifies self-worth and self-fulfillment, so has the church. . . .

"When the things of the world are idolized, as they frequently are even by believers, it is impossible not to be drawn into the moral and spiritual compromises that such idolatry demands. When a person longs to be like the world and insists on aping, he soon will be thinking and acting like it."

—*John MacArthur*

Reflecting on the Text

8) What standards should we expect or require of our spiritual and political leaders? How would you answer the argument that character and private conduct are irrelevant in choosing leaders?

_____

_____

9) Think about your life—your attitudes, values, behaviors. In what ways do you mirror the world? What needs to change so that your life stands in sharp contrast to our increasingly decadent culture?

_____

_____

_____

_____

10) In what situation has God placed you, like Samuel, to dissuade some of His people from making poor or worldly choices? How can you be faithful?

_____

_____

_____

_____

Recording Your Thoughts

Alicia - coworker's father had a heartattack, Wilhmina
Ginger's neighbor Tom lost his wife — fellowship!
Election./ Church elders election
Mary fell, needs support.
Derek - been depressed lately
Frank + Danielle - newly married

For further study, see the following passages:

Genesis 35:11	Numbers 24:7–9	Deuteronomy 16:19
Deuteronomy 17:14	Joshua 10:14	Joshua 12:7–24
Judges 2:18	Judges 17:6	1 Samuel 7:10
1 Kings 12:4		

Saul is Chosen as King!

1 Samuel 9:1—12:25

Opening Thought

1) Consider the following phrases:

"It's not how you start, it's how you finish."

"It's not over till it's over."

"All's well that ends well."

"The jury's still out."

"It's only half-time."

"Don't count your chickens before they hatch."

"There's many a slip between the cup and the lip."

"The opera ain't over till the fat lady sings."

All these sayings remind us of the danger of rendering a verdict or predicting an outcome too quickly. Events, situations, lives—all are capable of changing for better or worse.

What examples of this truth have you observed or experienced?

_____

_____

_____

Background of the Passage

During the time of the judges, Israel had been mired in sin and had suffered grievously as a result (often due to the Lord's discipline). When even the priests (that is, the house of Eli) became wicked, God raised up a young man named Samuel to lead His people. Both a judge and a prophet, the godly Samuel was able to exert a strong moral influence on the nation. As he aged, however, and as his own sons became corrupt, the elders of Israel made a bad decision.

They asked for a king so they could be like the other nations. They were, in effect, rejecting God, and Samuel told them so. Nevertheless God pledged to give them what they wanted.

Chapters 9—12 tell of the selection of Saul as king over Israel (9:1—10:16). A fine specimen of a man and from a well-to-do family of the tribe of Benjamin, Saul's reign gets off to a good start. The young king demonstrates humility (10:17–27) and leads the Israelites to a rousing military victory over the Ammonites (11:1–15).

Satisfied that He has fulfilled His ministry, Samuel delivers his farewell address to the nation (12:1–15). He gives a tribute to the Lord but also rebukes the people for their sin in wanting a human king. A supernatural lightning and rain storm authenticates Samuel's stern message and provides an ominous reminder that "It's not how you start, it's how you finish."

Bible Passage

Read 9:1—12:25, noting the key words and definitions to the right of the passage.

1 Samuel 9:1—12:25

1 There was a man of Benjamin whose name [was] Kish the son of Abiel, the son of Zeror, the son of Bechorath, the son of Aphiah, a Benjamite, a mighty man of power.

2 And he had a choice and handsome son whose name [was] Saul. [There was] not a more handsome person than he among the children of Israel. From his shoulders upward [he was] taller than any of the people.

3 Now the donkeys of Kish, Saul's father, were lost. And Kish said to his son Saul, "Please, take one of the servants with you, and arise, go and look for the donkeys."

4 So he passed through the mountains of Ephraim and through the land of Shalisha, but they did not find [them]. Then they passed through the land of Shaalim, and [they were] not [there]. Then he passed through the land of the Benjamites, but they did not find [them].

5 When they had come to the land of Zuph, Saul said to his servant who [was] with him, "Come, let us return, lest my father cease [caring] about the donkeys and become worried about us."

a mighty man of power (v. 1)—a man of wealth

choice and handsome (v. 2)— Emphasis was placed on a leader's stature and external appearance.

⁶ And he said to him, "Look now, [there is] in this city a man of God, and [he is] an honorable man; all that he says surely comes to pass. So let us go there; perhaps he can show us the way that we should go."

⁷ Then Saul said to his servant, "But look, [if] we go, what shall we bring the man? For the bread in our vessels is all gone, and [there is] no present to bring to the man of God. What do we have?"

⁸ And the servant answered Saul again and said, "Look, I have here at hand one fourth of a shekel of silver. I will give [that] to the man of God, to tell us our way."

⁹ (Formerly in Israel, when a man went to inquire of God, he spoke thus: "Come, let us go to the seer"; for [he who is] now [called] a prophet was formerly called a seer.)

¹⁰ Then Saul said to his servant, "Well said; come, let us go." So they went to the city where the man of God [was].

¹¹ As they went up the hill to the city, they met some young women going out to draw water, and said to them, "Is the seer here?"

¹² And they answered them and said, "Yes, there he is, just ahead of you. Hurry now; for today he came to this city, because there is a sacrifice of the people today on the high place.

¹³ "As soon as you come into the city, you will surely find him before he goes up to the high place to eat. For the people will not eat until he comes, because he must bless the sacrifice; afterward those who are invited will eat. Now therefore, go up, for about this time you will find him."

¹⁴ So they went up to the city. As they were coming into the city, there was Samuel, coming out toward them on his way up to the high place.

¹⁵ Now the LORD had told Samuel in his ear the day before Saul came, saying,

¹⁶ "Tomorrow about this time I will send you a man from the land of Benjamin, and you shall anoint him commander over My people Israel, that he may save My people from the hand of the Philistines; for I have looked upon My people, because their cry has come to me."

¹⁷ And when Samuel saw Saul, the LORD said to him, "There he is, the man of whom I spoke to you. This one shall reign over My people."

¹⁸ Then Saul drew near to Samuel in the gate, and said, "Please tell me, where [is] the seer's house?"

¹⁹ And Samuel answered Saul and said, "I [am] the seer. Go up before me to the high place, for you

a man of God (v. 6)—a description of the prophet and judge Samuel

no present to bring (v. 7)—It was customary to bring a gift of gratitude to a prophet.

a prophet was formerly called a seer (v. 9)—due to his God-given ability to "see" the future

high place (v. 12)—Essentially Canaanite in background, these religious sites for worship and sacrifice were constructed so that onlookers could see the sacrifices being offered for them.

anoint him (v. 16)—representing a setting apart for service to the Lord

commander (v. 16)—literally "one given prominence"; that is, one designated to rule

This one (v. 17)—God was clearly identifying Saul to Samuel.

shall eat with me today; and tomorrow I will let you go and will tell you all that [is] in your heart.

20 "But as for your donkeys that were lost three days ago, do not be anxious about them, for they have been found. And on whom [is] all the desire of Israel? [Is it] not on you and on all your father's house?"

21 And Saul answered and said, "[Am] I not a Benjamite, of the smallest of the tribes of Israel, and my family the least of all the families of the tribe of Benjamin? Why then do you speak like this to me?"

22 Now Samuel took Saul and his servant and brought them into the hall, and had them sit in the place of honor among those who were invited; there [were] about thirty persons.

23 And Samuel said to the cook, "Bring the portion which I gave you, of which I said to you, 'Set it apart.'"

24 So the cook took up the thigh with its upper part and set [it] before Saul. And [Samuel] said, "Here it is, what was kept back. [It] was set apart for you. Eat; for until this time it has been kept for you, since I said I invited the people." So Saul ate with Samuel that day.

25 When they had come down from the high place into the city, [Samuel] spoke with Saul on the top of the house.

26 They arose early; and it was about the dawning of the day that Samuel called to Saul on the top of the house, saying, "Get up, that I may send you on your way." And Saul arose, and both of them went outside, he and Samuel.

27 As they were going down to the outskirts of the city, Samuel said to Saul, "Tell the servant to go on ahead of us." And he went on. "But you stand here awhile, that I may announce to you the word of God."

1 Then Samuel took a flask of oil and poured [it] on his head, and kissed him and said: "[Is it] not because the LORD has anointed you commander over His inheritance?

2 "When you have departed from me today, you will find two men by Rachel's tomb in the territory of Benjamin at Zelzah; and they will say to you, 'The donkeys which you went to look for have been found. And now your father has ceased caring about the donkeys and is worrying about you, saying, "What shall I do about my son?"'

3 "Then you shall go on forward from there and

a Benjamite . . . the least of all the families (v. 21)—Saul's humility and timidity can be seen in his proper assessment of his tribe.

the thigh . . . set apart for you (v. 24)—Being given the choice meat was indicative of Saul's new status.

His inheritance (10:1)—Israel was God's unique possession.

come to the terebinth tree of Tabor. There three men going up to God at Bethel will meet you, one carrying three young goats, another carrying three loaves of bread, and another carrying a skin of wine.

4 "And they will greet you and give you two [loaves] of bread, which you shall receive from their hands.

5 "After that you shall come to the hill of God where the Philistine garrison [is]. And it will happen, when you have come there to the city, that you will meet a group of prophets coming down from the high place with a stringed instrument, a tambourine, a flute, and a harp before them; and they will be prophesying.

6 "Then the Spirit of the LORD will come upon you, and you will prophesy with them and be turned into another man.

7 "And let it be, when these signs come to you, [that] you do as the occasion demands; for God [is] with you.

8 "You shall go down before me to Gilgal; and surely I will come down to you to offer burnt offerings [and] make sacrifices of peace offerings. Seven days you shall wait, till I come to you and show you what you should do."

9 So it was, when he had turned his back to go from Samuel, that God gave him another heart; and all those signs came to pass that day.

10 When they came there to the hill, there was a group of prophets to meet him; then the Spirit of God came upon him, and he prophesied among them.

11 And it happened, when all who knew him formerly saw that he indeed prophesied among the prophets, that the people said to one another, "What [is] this [that] has come upon the son of Kish? [Is] Saul also among the prophets?"

12 Then a man from there answered and said, "But who [is] their father?" Therefore it became a proverb: "[Is] Saul also among the prophets?"

13 And when he had finished prophesying, he went to the high place.

14 Then Saul's uncle said to him and his servant, "Where did you go?" So he said, "To look for the donkeys. When we saw that [they were] nowhere [to be found], we went to Samuel."

15 And Saul's uncle said, "Tell me, please, what Samuel said to you."

16 So Saul said to his uncle, "He told us plainly that the donkeys had been found." But about the matter of the kingdom, he did not tell him what Samuel had said.

a group of prophets (v. 5)— young men being trained by Samuel for prophetic ministry

turned into another man (v. 6)—With the empowerment of the Holy Spirit, Saul would emerge a new man, equipped to lead.

God gave him another heart (v. 9)—God prepared Saul for the kingship by having the Holy Spirit come upon him.

17 Then Samuel called the people together to the LORD at Mizpah,

18 and said to the children of Israel, "Thus says the LORD God of Israel: 'I brought up Israel out of Egypt, and delivered you from the hand of the Egyptians [and] from the hand of all kingdoms and from those who oppressed you.'

19 "But you have today rejected your God, who Himself saved you from all your adversities and your tribulations; and you have said to Him, 'No, set a king over us!' Now therefore, present yourselves before the LORD by your tribes and by your clans."

20 And when Samuel had caused all the tribes of Israel to come near, the tribe of Benjamin was chosen.

21 When he had caused the tribe of Benjamin to come near by their families, the family of Matri was chosen. And Saul the son of Kish was chosen. But when they sought him, he could not be found.

22 Therefore they inquired of the LORD further, "Has the man come here yet?" And the LORD answered, "There he is, hidden among the equipment."

23 So they ran and brought him from there; and when he stood among the people, he was taller than any of the people from his shoulders upward.

24 And Samuel said to all the people, "Do you see him whom the LORD has chosen, that [there is] no one like him among all the people?" So all the people shouted and said, "Long live the king!"

25 Then Samuel explained to the people the behavior of royalty, and wrote [it] in a book and laid [it] up before the LORD. And Samuel sent all the people away, every man to his house.

26 And Saul also went home to Gibeah; and valiant [men] went with him, whose hearts God had touched.

27 But some rebels said, "How can this man save us?" So they despised him, and brought him no presents. But he held his peace.

1 Then Nahash the Ammonite came up and encamped against Jabesh Gilead; and all the men of Jabesh said to Nahash, "Make a covenant with us, and we will serve you."

2 And Nahash the Ammonite answered them, "On this [condition] I will make [a covenant] with you, that I may put out all your right eyes, and bring reproach on all Israel."

3 Then the elders of Jabesh said to him, "Hold off for

Samuel called the people (v. 17)—to make public the Lord's choice of Saul

chosen (vv. 20–21)—Probably lots were cast before the people to confirm God's selection.

hidden among the equipment (v. 22)—Saul was overwhelmed and likely fearful.

behavior of royalty (v. 25)— the regulations for kings according to Deuteronomy 17

whose hearts God had touched (v. 26)—valiant men eager to affirm God's choice and divinely prompted to join him

put out all your right eyes (11:2)—a barbarous mutilation practiced in the ancient Near East so as to disable a warrior's depth perception and peripheral vision, thus rendering him useless for battle

seven days, that we may send messengers to all the territory of Israel. And then, if [there is] no one to save us, we will come out to you."

4 So the messengers came to Gibeah of Saul and told the news in the hearing of the people. And all the people lifted up their voices and wept.

5 Now there was Saul, coming behind the herd from the field; and Saul said, "What [troubles] the people, that they weep?" And they told him the words of the men of Jabesh.

6 Then the Spirit of God came upon Saul when he heard this news, and his anger was greatly aroused.

7 So he took a yoke of oxen and cut them in pieces, and sent [them] throughout all the territory of Israel by the hands of messengers, saying, "Whoever does not go out with Saul and Samuel to battle, so it shall be done to his oxen." And the fear of the LORD fell on the people, and they came out with one consent.

8 When he numbered them in Bezek, the children of Israel were three hundred thousand, and the men of Judah thirty thousand.

9 And they said to the messengers who came, "Thus you shall say to the men of Jabesh Gilead: 'Tomorrow, by [the time] the sun is hot, you shall have help.'" Then the messengers came and reported [it] to the men of Jabesh, and they were glad.

10 Therefore the men of Jabesh said, "Tomorrow we will come out to you, and you may do with us whatever seems good to you."

11 So it was, on the next day, that Saul put the people in three companies; and they came into the midst of the camp in the morning watch, and killed Ammonites until the heat of the day. And it happened that those who survived were scattered, so that no two of them were left together.

12 Then the people said to Samuel, "Who [is] he who said, 'Shall Saul reign over us?' Bring the men, that we may put them to death."

13 But Saul said, "Not a man shall be put to death this day, for today the LORD has accomplished salvation in Israel."

14 Then Samuel said to the people, "Come, let us go to Gilgal and renew the kingdom there."

15 So all the people went to Gilgal, and there they made Saul king before the LORD in Gilgal. There they made sacrifices of peace offerings before the LORD, and there Saul and all the men of Israel rejoiced greatly.

from the field (v. 5)—Saul continued to work as a farmer while awaiting kingly responsibilities and expectations.

three companies (v. 11)—a military strategy of dividing up one's force to give more options and prevent a total loss

the Lord has accomplished salvation (v. 13)—Saul gave God the credit and refused to use the occasion to execute his detractors.

they made Saul king (v. 15)—a public coronation and celebration

¹ Now Samuel said to all Israel: "Indeed I have heeded your voice in all that you said to me, and have made a king over you.

² "And now here is the king, walking before you; and I am old and grayheaded, and look, my sons [are] with you. I have walked before you from my childhood to this day.

³ "Here I am. Witness against me before the LORD and before His anointed: Whose ox have I taken, or whose donkey have I taken, or whom have I cheated? Whom have I oppressed, or from whose hand have I received [any] bribe with which to blind my eyes? I will restore [it] to you."

⁴ And they said, "You have not cheated us or oppressed us, nor have you taken anything from any man's hand."

⁵ Then he said to them, "The LORD [is] witness against you, and His anointed [is] witness this day, that you have not found anything in my hand." And they answered, "[He is] witness."

⁶ Then Samuel said to the people, "[It is] the LORD who raised up Moses and Aaron, and who brought your fathers up from the land of Egypt.

⁷ "Now therefore, stand still, that I may reason with you before the LORD concerning all the righteous acts of the LORD which He did to you and your fathers:

⁸ "When Jacob had gone into Egypt, and your fathers cried out to the LORD, then the LORD sent Moses and Aaron, who brought your fathers out of Egypt and made them dwell in this place.

⁹ "And when they forgot the LORD their God, He sold them into the hand of Sisera, commander of the army of Hazor, into the hand of the Philistines, and into the hand of the king of Moab; and they fought against them.

¹⁰ "Then they cried out to the LORD, and said, 'We have sinned, because we have forsaken the LORD and served the Baals and Ashtoreths; but now deliver us from the hand of our enemies, and we will serve You.'

¹¹ "And the LORD sent Jerubbaal, Bedan, Jephthah, and Samuel, and delivered you out of the hand of your enemies on every side; and you dwelt in safety.

¹² "And when you saw that Nahash king of the Ammonites came against you, you said to me, 'No, but a king shall reign over us,' when the LORD your God [was] your king.

¹³ "Now therefore, here is the king whom you have chosen [and] whom you have desired. And take note, the LORD has set a king over you.

I have heeded your voice
(12:1)—Samuel obeyed the will of the people and the command of the Lord in giving them a king.

Here I am (v. 3)—symbolic of Samuel's availability to God and the people

I may reason with you (v. 7)—Samuel's final warning and rebuke of the people

the Lord was your king
(v. 12)—the clearest indictment of Israel for choosing a mere man to fight for her rather than God

¹⁴ *"If you fear the LORD and serve Him and obey His voice, and do not rebel against the commandment of the LORD, then both you and the king who reigns over you will continue following the LORD your God.*

¹⁵ *"However, if you do not obey the voice of the LORD, but rebel against the commandment of the LORD, then the hand of the LORD will be against you, as [it was] against your fathers.*

¹⁶ *"Now therefore, stand and see this great thing which the LORD will do before your eyes:*

¹⁷ *"[Is] today not the wheat harvest? I will call to the LORD, and He will send thunder and rain, that you may perceive and see that your wickedness [is] great, which you have done in the sight of the LORD, in asking a king for yourselves."*

¹⁸ *So Samuel called to the LORD, and the LORD sent thunder and rain that day; and all the people greatly feared the LORD and Samuel.*

¹⁹ *And all the people said to Samuel, "Pray for your servants to the LORD your God, that we may not die; for we have added to all our sins the evil of asking a king for ourselves."*

²⁰ *Then Samuel said to the people, "Do not fear. You have done all this wickedness; yet do not turn aside from following the LORD, but serve the LORD with all your heart.*

²¹ *"And do not turn aside; for [then you would go] after empty things which cannot profit or deliver, for they [are] nothing.*

²² *"For the LORD will not forsake His people, for His great name's sake, because it has pleased the LORD to make you His people.*

²³ *"Moreover, as for me, far be it from me that I should sin against the LORD in ceasing to pray for you; but I will teach you the good and the right way.*

²⁴ *"Only fear the LORD, and serve Him in truth with all your heart; for consider what great things He has done for you.*

²⁵ *"But if you still do wickedly, you shall be swept away, both you and your king."*

fear the Lord (v. 14)—Israel was to stand in awe of the Lord and submit to Him.

rebel (v. 15)—disobey, not heed, forsake; blessings would follow obedience, curses would follow disobedience

this great thing (v. 16)—Thunder and lightning during the wheat harvest were so unusual that the people recognized this event as a divine sign.

empty things (v. 21)—literally "futile things," that is, idols

Understanding the Text

2) How did God lead Samuel to Saul and Saul to Samuel? What first impressions does the text give us of Saul?

_____

_____

3) How did God supernaturally confirm His choice of Saul?

_____

_____

_____

4) What was the people's initial reaction to the choice of Saul as king? What event(s) happened to galvanize public support for his reign?

_____

_____

_____

Cross-Reference

Compare the standards for kings in Deuteronomy 17 to what you just read.

Deuteronomy 17:14–20
¹⁴ *"When you come to the land which the LORD your God is giving you, and possess it and dwell in it, and say, 'I will set a king over me like all the nations that [are] around me,'*

¹⁵ *"you shall surely set a king over you whom the LORD your God chooses; [one] from among your brethren you shall set as king over you; you may not set a foreigner over you, who [is] not your brother.*

¹⁶ *"But he shall not multiply horses for himself, nor cause the people to return to Egypt to multiply horses, for the LORD has said to you, 'You shall not return that way again.'*

¹⁷ *"Neither shall he multiply wives for himself, lest his heart turn away; nor shall he greatly multiply silver and gold for himself.*

¹⁸ *"Also it shall be, when he sits on the throne of his kingdom, that he shall write for himself a copy of this law in a book, from [the one] before the priests, the Levites.*

¹⁹ *"And it shall be with him, and he shall read it all the days of his life, that he may learn to fear the LORD his God and be careful to observe all the words of this law and these statutes,*

²⁰ *"that his heart may not be lifted above his brethren, that he may not turn aside from the commandment [to] the right hand or [to] the left, and that he may prolong [his] days in his kingdom, he and his children in the midst of Israel.*

Exploring the Meaning

5) Why do you suppose the Mosaic Law contains *these* particular commands for kings? What wisdom do you see in them?

_____

_____

6) In the Old Testament, the Holy Spirit came upon individuals temporarily to empower them for special acts of service (for example, 10:6). In the case of flagrant sin, God would also withdraw His Spirit (16:14; Psalm 51:11). What New Testament promises say that God's Spirit will be in us always?

_____

_____

7) How did the Israelites feel following Samuel's address at the coronation of Saul? Why?

_____

_____

Summing Up . . .

"God has always been concerned above all else with the inside of a man, with the condition of his heart. When the Lord called Saul to be Israel's first king, 'God changed his heart' (10:9). Until then Saul had been handsome, athletic, and not much more. But the new king soon began to revert to his old heart patterns. He chose to disobey God and to trust in himself. . . . God took the kingdom from Saul because he refused to live by the new heart God had given him." —*John MacArthur*

Reflecting on the Text

8) If all you knew about the life of Saul was the information you have in chapters 9—12, what conclusions would you draw about his character?

If you did not have the benefit of the historical record of chapters 13—31, what predictions might you make about his future reign?

What does this imply about "counting chickens before they're hatched?"

_____

_____

9) Someone has said that, "The one thing worse than not getting what you want is *getting* it." How does this bit of wisdom apply to Israel and their demand for a king?

_____

_____

10) What practical steps can you make or take today to help insure you finish strong in the Christian life?

_____

_____

Recording Your Thoughts

_____

_____

_____

_____

_____

For further study, see the following passages:

Genesis 49:10	Exodus 2:25	Deuteronomy 4:20
Deuteronomy 10:12	Deuteronomy 12:2–5	Joshua 14:14
Judges 6:34	Judges 19:29	Ruth 2:1
2 Samuel 7:5	1 Kings 1:35	1 Kings 14:3
1 Chronicles 25:1	Psalm 106:15	Ecclesiastes 9:10

The Reign of Saul

Opening Thought

1) The Biblical standard for believers (and *especially* for those who would lead others spiritually) is nothing short of holiness. Yet in a tolerant society with lax morals and few standards, Christians often settle for partial obedience. Or they participate in a few good deeds (church attendance, Bible reading, and so forth) in an attempt to offset their questionable behaviors or pet vices.

What are the consequences when the people of God tolerate sin and downplay acts of unrighteousness?

_____

_____

2) What happens when the people of God try to maintain (for themselves and for their culture) high standards of purity and faithfulness?

_____

_____

Background of the Passage

At the coronation of Saul, Samuel had concluded his remarks with a sober warning to both the new king and the nation, "Only fear the Lord, and serve Him in truth with all your heart; for consider what great things He has done for you. But if you still do wickedly, you shall be swept away, both you and your king" (12:24–25). Despite this dire warning and a fairly successful start as Israel's monarch, Saul quickly proved himself unfit to lead through a series of rebellious choices and high-handed acts. In chapter 13, Saul demonstrated flagrant disbelief by assuming Samuel's role as priest. From this act there would be no political redemption or rehabilitation. The prophet immediately announced Saul's unfitness and God's rejection of Saul as king. The rest of Saul's reign is one sad example after another of a man trying to discharge service to God without the blessing of God.

In chapter 14, a great victory by Jonathan (the son of the king) is overshadowed by an impulsive oath by Saul. This is yet another indication of Saul's unkingly character.

In chapter 15, Saul disregards the clear command of the Lord to completely annihilate the enemy Amalekites. In a very public fashion, the kingdom is symbolically ripped from Saul, and to further illustrate Saul's alienation from God, Samuel separates himself from the self-willed king.

Bible Passage

Read 13:1—15:35, noting the key words and definitions to the right of the passage.

1 Samuel 13:1—15:35

1 Saul reigned one year; and when he had reigned two years over Israel,

2 Saul chose for himself three thousand [men] of Israel. Two thousand were with Saul in Michmash and in the mountains of Bethel, and a thousand were with Jonathan in Gibeah of Benjamin. The rest of the people he sent away, every man to his tent.

3 And Jonathan attacked the garrison of the Philistines that [was] in Geba, and the Philistines heard [of it]. Then Saul blew the trumpet throughout all the land, saying, "Let the Hebrews hear!"

4 Now all Israel heard it said [that] Saul had attacked a garrison of the Philistines, and [that] Israel had also become an abomination to the Philistines. And the people were called together to Saul at Gilgal.

5 Then the Philistines gathered together to fight with Israel, thirty thousand chariots and six thousand horsemen, and people as the sand which [is] on the seashore in multitude. And they came up and encamped in Michmash, to the east of Beth Aven.

6 When the men of Israel saw that they were in danger (for the people were distressed), then the people hid in caves, in thickets, in rocks, in holes, and in pits.

7 And [some of] the Hebrews crossed over the Jordan to

Jonathan (v. 2)—Saul's firstborn son and heir apparent to the throne

abomination (v. 4)—The Philistines hated Israel, and Israel could expect retaliation for Jonathan's attack.

the land of Gad and Gilead. As for Saul, he [was] still in Gilgal, and all the people followed him trembling.

8 Then he waited seven days, according to the time set by Samuel. But Samuel did not come to Gilgal; and the people were scattered from him.

9 So Saul said, "Bring a burnt offering and peace offerings here to me." And he offered the burnt offering.

10 Now it happened, as soon as he had finished presenting the burnt offering, that Samuel came; and Saul went out to meet him, that he might greet him.

11 And Samuel said, "What have you done?" And Saul said, "When I saw that the people were scattered from me, and [that] you did not come within the days appointed, and [that] the Philistines gathered together at Michmash,

12 "then I said, 'The Philistines will now come down on me at Gilgal, and I have not made supplication to the LORD.' Therefore I felt compelled, and offered a burnt offering."

13 And Samuel said to Saul, "You have done foolishly. You have not kept the commandment of the LORD your God, which He commanded you. For now the LORD would have established your kingdom over Israel forever.

14 "But now your kingdom shall not continue. The LORD has sought for Himself a man after His own heart, and the LORD has commanded him [to be] commander over His people, because you have not kept what the LORD commanded you."

15 Then Samuel arose and went up from Gilgal to Gibeah of Benjamin. And Saul numbered the people present with him, about six hundred men.

16 Saul, Jonathan his son, and the people present with them remained in Gibeah of Benjamin. But the Philistines encamped in Michmash.

17 Then raiders came out of the camp of the Philistines in three companies. One company turned to the road to Ophrah, to the land of Shual,

18 another company turned to the road [to] Beth Horon, and another company turned [to] the road of the border that overlooks the Valley of Zeboim toward the wilderness.

19 Now there was no blacksmith to be found throughout all the land of Israel, for the Philistines said, "Lest the Hebrews make swords or spears."

20 But all the Israelites would go down to the Philistines to sharpen each man's plowshare, his mattock, his ax, and his sickle;

21 and the charge for a sharpening was a pim for the plowshares, the mattocks, the forks, and the axes, and to set the points of the goads.

22 So it came about, on the day of battle, that there was neither sword nor spear found in the hand of any of

trembling (v. 7)—The people feared a certain Philistine reprisal.

the time set by Samuel (v. 8)—Saul had been commanded (10:8) to wait seven days for Samuel at Gilgal.

the people were scattered (v. 8)—Saul's troops began going AWOL.

he offered the burnt offering (v. 9)—Saul refused to wait for Samuel and assumed the priestly role for himself.

When I saw (v. 11)—an example of walking by sight instead of by faith

a man after His own heart (v. 14)—This refers to David who had the desire and will to obey God.

no blacksmith (v. 19)—The Philistines had superior iron and metal-working craftsmen until David's time, accounting for their military might.

mattocks (v. 20)—pickaxes

neither sword nor spear (v. 21)—The Israelites were forced to fight with farm implements.

the people who [were] with Saul and Jonathan. But they were found with Saul and Jonathan his son.

23 And the garrison of the Philistines went out to the pass of Michmash.

1 Now it happened one day that Jonathan the son of Saul said to the young man who bore his armor, "Come, let us go over to the Philistines' garrison that [is] on the other side." But he did not tell his father.

2 And Saul was sitting in the outskirts of Gibeah under a pomegranate tree which [is] in Migron. The people who [were] with him [were] about six hundred men.

3 Ahijah the son of Ahitub, Ichabod's brother, the son of Phinehas, the son of Eli, the LORD's priest in Shiloh, was wearing an ephod. But the people did not know that Jonathan had gone.

4 Between the passes, by which Jonathan sought to go over to the Philistines' garrison, [there was] a sharp rock on one side and a sharp rock on the other side. And the name of one [was] Bozez, and the name of the other Seneh.

5 The front of one faced northward opposite Michmash, and the other southward opposite Gibeah.

6 Then Jonathan said to the young man who bore his armor, "Come, let us go over to the garrison of these uncircumcised; it may be that the LORD will work for us. For nothing restrains the LORD from saving by many or by few."

7 So his armorbearer said to him, "Do all that is in your heart. Go then; here I am with you, according to your heart."

8 Then Jonathan said, "Very well, let us cross over to [these] men, and we will show ourselves to them.

9 "If they say thus to us, 'Wait until we come to you,' then we will stand still in our place and not go up to them.

10 "But if they say thus, 'Come up to us,' then we will go up. For the LORD has delivered them into our hand, and this [will be] a sign to us."

11 So both of them showed themselves to the garrison of the Philistines. And the Philistines said, "Look, the Hebrews are coming out of the holes where they have hidden."

12 Then the men of the garrison called to Jonathan and his armorbearer, and said, "Come up to us, and we will show you something." Jonathan said to his armorbearer, "Come up after me, for the LORD has delivered them into the hand of Israel."

13 And Jonathan climbed up on his hands and knees with his armorbearer after him; and they fell before Jonathan. And as he came after him, his armorbearer killed them.

14 That first slaughter which Jonathan and his armor-

uncircumcised (14:6)—a derogatory term used by the Jews to describe God's enemies

by many or few (v. 6)—illustrative of Jonathan's faith

a sign to us (v. 10)—an unorthodox means of determining God's will

bearer made was about twenty men within about half an acre of land.

15 And there was trembling in the camp, in the field, and among all the people. The garrison and the raiders also trembled; and the earth quaked, so that it was a very great trembling.

16 Now the watchmen of Saul in Gibeah of Benjamin looked, and [there] was the multitude, melting away; and they went here and there.

17 Then Saul said to the people who [were] with him, "Now call the roll and see who has gone from us." And when they had called the roll, surprisingly, Jonathan and his armorbearer [were] not [there].

18 And Saul said to Ahijah, "Bring the ark of God here" (for at that time the ark of God was with the children of Israel).

19 Now it happened, while Saul talked to the priest, that the noise which [was] in the camp of the Philistines continued to increase; so Saul said to the priest, "Withdraw your hand."

20 Then Saul and all the people who [were] with him assembled, and they went to the battle; and indeed every man's sword was against his neighbor, [and there was] very great confusion.

21 Moreover the Hebrews [who] were with the Philistines before that time, who went up with them into the camp [from the] surrounding [country], they also joined the Israelites who [were] with Saul and Jonathan.

22 Likewise all the men of Israel who had hidden in the mountains of Ephraim, [when] they heard that the Philistines fled, they also followed hard after them in the battle.

23 So the LORD saved Israel that day, and the battle shifted to Beth Aven.

24 And the men of Israel were distressed that day, for Saul had placed the people under oath, saying, "Cursed [is] the man who eats [any] food until evening, before I have taken vengeance on my enemies." So none of the people tasted food.

25 Now all [the people] of the land came to a forest; and there was honey on the ground.

26 And when the people had come into the woods, there was the honey, dripping; but no one put his hand to his mouth, for the people feared the oath.

27 But Jonathan had not heard his father charge the people with the oath; therefore he stretched out the end of the rod that [was] in his hand and dipped it in a honeycomb, and put his hand to his mouth; and his countenance brightened.

28 Then one of the people said, "Your father strictly charged the people with an oath, saying, 'Cursed [is]

the earth quaked (v. 15)— Divine intervention made possible Jonathan's military success.

Withdraw your hand (v. 19)— Saul, in a hurry, ordered the priest to stop the inquiry into God's will.

were distressed (v. 24)—Saul's inept leadership failed to provide for the physical needs of his men, leaving them weak and fatigued.

Cursed (v. 24)—Saul's foolish oath forbade eating until the battle was over; it was made just after Jonathan's departure, so that he had not heard it.

honey on the ground (v. 25)— honeycombs found in the forest

the man who eats food this day.'" And the people were faint.

29 But Jonathan said, "My father has troubled the land. Look now, how my countenance has brightened because I tasted a little of this honey.

30 "How much better if the people had eaten freely today of the spoil of their enemies which they found! For now would there not have been a much greater slaughter among the Philistines?"

31 Now they had driven back the Philistines that day from Michmash to Aijalon. So the people were very faint.

32 And the people rushed on the spoil, and took sheep, oxen, and calves, and slaughtered [them] on the ground; and the people ate [them] with the blood.

33 Then they told Saul, saying, "Look, the people are sinning against the LORD by eating with the blood!" So he said, "You have dealt treacherously; roll a large stone to me this day."

34 And Saul said, "Disperse yourselves among the people, and say to them, 'Bring me here every man's ox and every man's sheep, slaughter [them] here, and eat; and do not sin against the LORD by eating with the blood.'" So every one of the people brought his ox with him that night, and slaughtered [it] there.

35 Then Saul built an altar to the LORD. This was the first altar that he built to the LORD.

36 Now Saul said, "Let us go down after the Philistines by night, and plunder them until the morning light; and let us not leave a man of them." And they said, "Do whatever seems good to you." Then the priest said, "Let us draw near to God here."

37 So Saul asked counsel of God, "Shall I go down after the Philistines? Will You deliver them into the hand of Israel?" But He did not answer him that day.

38 And Saul said, "Come over here, all you chiefs of the people, and know and see what this sin was today.

39 "For [as] the LORD lives, who saves Israel, though it be in Jonathan my son, he shall surely die." But not a man among all the people answered him.

40 Then he said to all Israel, "You be on one side, and my son Jonathan and I will be on the other side." And the people said to Saul, "Do what seems good to you."

41 Therefore Saul said to the LORD God of Israel, "Give a perfect [lot]." So Saul and Jonathan were taken, but the people escaped.

42 And Saul said, "Cast [lots] between my son Jonathan and me." So Jonathan was taken.

43 Then Saul said to Jonathan, "Tell me what you have done." And Jonathan told him, and said, "I only tasted a little honey with the end of the rod that [was] in my hand. So now I must die!"

ate them with the blood
(v. 32)—The famished men disobeyed the law by not properly draining the blood from the meat before eating it.

He did not answer him
(v. 37)—The Lord refused to respond to the sinful Saul.

as the Lord lives (v. 39)—another foolish oath, endangering his own son's life

44 And Saul answered, "God do so and more also; for you shall surely die, Jonathan."

45 But the people said to Saul, "Shall Jonathan die, who has accomplished this great deliverance in Israel? Certainly not! [As] the LORD lives, not one hair of his head shall fall to the ground, for he has worked with God this day." So the people rescued Jonathan, and he did not die.

46 Then Saul returned from pursuing the Philistines, and the Philistines went to their own place.

47 So Saul established his sovereignty over Israel, and fought against all his enemies on every side, against Moab, against the people of Ammon, against Edom, against the kings of Zobah, and against the Philistines. Wherever he turned, he harassed [them].

48 And he gathered an army and attacked the Amalekites, and delivered Israel from the hands of those who plundered them.

49 The sons of Saul were Jonathan, Jishui and Malchishua. And the names of his two daughters [were these]: the name of the firstborn Merab, and the name of the younger Michal.

50 The name of Saul's wife [was] Ahinoam the daughter of Ahimaaz. And the name of the commander of his army [was] Abner the son of Ner, Saul's uncle.

51 Kish [was] the father of Saul, and Ner the father of Abner [was] the son of Abiel.

52 Now there was fierce war with the Philistines all the days of Saul. And when Saul saw any strong man or any valiant man, he took him for himself.

1 Samuel also said to Saul, "The LORD sent me to anoint you king over His people, over Israel. Now therefore, heed the voice of the words of the LORD.

2 "Thus says the LORD of hosts: 'I will punish Amalek [for] what he did to Israel, how he ambushed him on the way when he came up from Egypt.

3 'Now go and attack Amalek, and utterly destroy all that they have, and do not spare them. But kill both man and woman, infant and nursing child, ox and sheep, camel and donkey.'"

4 So Saul gathered the people together and numbered them in Telaim, two hundred thousand foot soldiers and ten thousand men of Judah.

5 And Saul came to a city of Amalek, and lay in wait in the valley.

6 Then Saul said to the Kenites, "Go, depart, get down from among the Amalekites, lest I destroy you with them. For you showed kindness to all the children of Israel when they came up out of Egypt." So the Kenites departed from among the Amalekites.

7 And Saul attacked the Amalekites, from Havilah all the way to Shur, which is east of Egypt.

God do so and more also (v. 44)—Proud Saul was determined to carry out his vow to prove his authority.

Abner (v. 50)—Saul's cousin and commander of his army

took him for himself (v. 52)—Saul added every able warrior he could find to his personal force.

Amalek (15:2)—nomadic desert peoples descended from Esau who had attacked Israel upon her departure from Egypt

utterly destroy (v. 3)—Complete judgment was decreed for those who would seek to destroy God's people.

⁸ He also took Agag king of the Amalekites alive, and utterly destroyed all the people with the edge of the sword.

⁹ But Saul and the people spared Agag and the best of the sheep, the oxen, the fatlings, the lambs, and all [that was] good, and were unwilling to utterly destroy them. But everything despised and worthless, that they utterly destroyed.

¹⁰ Now the word of the LORD came to Samuel, saying,

¹¹ "I greatly regret that I have set up Saul [as] king, for he has turned back from following Me, and has not performed My commandments." And it grieved Samuel, and he cried out to the LORD all night.

¹² So when Samuel rose early in the morning to meet Saul, it was told Samuel, saying, "Saul went to Carmel, and indeed, he set up a monument for himself; and he has gone on around, passed by, and gone down to Gilgal."

¹³ Then Samuel went to Saul, and Saul said to him, "Blessed [are] you of the LORD! I have performed the commandment of the LORD."

¹⁴ But Samuel said, "What then [is] this bleating of the sheep in my ears, and the lowing of the oxen which I hear?"

¹⁵ And Saul said, "They have brought them from the Amalekites; for the people spared the best of the sheep and the oxen, to sacrifice to the LORD your God; and the rest we have utterly destroyed."

¹⁶ Then Samuel said to Saul, "Be quiet! And I will tell you what the LORD said to me last night." And he said to him, "Speak on."

¹⁷ So Samuel said, "When you [were] little in your own eyes, [were] you not head of the tribes of Israel? And did not the LORD anoint you king over Israel?

¹⁸ "Now the LORD sent you on a mission, and said, 'Go, and utterly destroy the sinners, the Amalekites, and fight against them until they are consumed.'

¹⁹ "Why then did you not obey the voice of the LORD? Why did you swoop down on the spoil, and do evil in the sight of the LORD?"

²⁰ And Saul said to Samuel, "But I have obeyed the voice of the LORD, and gone on the mission on which the LORD sent me, and brought back Agag king of Amalek; I have utterly destroyed the Amalekites.

²¹ "But the people took of the plunder, sheep and oxen, the best of the things which should have been utterly destroyed, to sacrifice to the LORD your God in Gilgal."

²² Then Samuel said: "Has the LORD [as great] delight in burnt offerings and sacrifices, As in obeying the voice of the LORD? Behold, to obey is better than sacrifice, [And] to heed than the fat of rams.

²³ For rebellion [is as] the sin of witchcraft, And stub-

Agag . . . and the best of the sheep (vv. 8–9)—Saul took it upon himself to spare the king of the Amalekites and some of the choice livestock.

monument for himself (v. 12)—Saul was claiming credit for the victory.

I have performed the commandment of the Lord (v. 13)—proof either of Saul's delusion or his deceptive nature

the people . . . to sacrifice (v. 15)—Saul first attempted to pin the blame on others; then he tried to excuse the disobedience by claiming that the ends justify the means.

I have obeyed (vv. 20–21)—Saul's continued rationalization and justification of his sin

to obey is better than sacrifice (v. 22)—God desires heart obedience and true submission more than religious rituals and empty acts of service.

bornness [is as] iniquity and idolatry. Because you have rejected the word of the LORD, He also has rejected you from [being] king."

24 Then Saul said to Samuel, "I have sinned, for I have transgressed the commandment of the LORD and your words, because I feared the people and obeyed their voice.

25 "Now therefore, please pardon my sin, and return with me, that I may worship the LORD."

26 But Samuel said to Saul, "I will not return with you, for you have rejected the word of the LORD, and the LORD has rejected you from being king over Israel."

27 And as Samuel turned around to go away, [Saul] seized the edge of his robe, and it tore.

28 So Samuel said to him, "The LORD has torn the kingdom of Israel from you today, and has given it to a neighbor of yours, [who is] better than you.

29 "And also the Strength of Israel will not lie nor relent. For He [is] not a man, that He should relent."

30 Then he said, "I have sinned; [yet] honor me now, please, before the elders of my people and before Israel, and return with me, that I may worship the LORD your God."

31 So Samuel turned back after Saul, and Saul worshiped the LORD.

32 Then Samuel said, "Bring Agag king of the Amalekites here to me." So Agag came to him cautiously. And Agag said, "Surely the bitterness of death is past."

33 But Samuel said, "As your sword has made women childless, so shall your mother be childless among women." And Samuel hacked Agag in pieces before the LORD in Gilgal.

34 Then Samuel went to Ramah, and Saul went up to his house at Gibeah of Saul.

35 And Samuel went no more to see Saul until the day of his death. Nevertheless Samuel mourned for Saul, and the LORD regretted that He had made Saul king over Israel.

I have sinned (v. 24)—This overdue confession seems motivated more by a concern over consequences than by the sorrow of having offended holy God; again it drifts toward blame.

return with me . . . honor me (v. 25, 30)—Saul wanted Samuel's visible support to prop up his collapsing regime and help him look good in the eyes of the people.

torn the kingdom (v. 28)—The torn robe became an illustration of God tearing the kingdom away from the disobedient monarch.

hacked Agag in pieces (v. 33)—This act of divine judgment demonstrated God's holy wrath against wanton sin.

Understanding the Text

3) What was Saul's rationale for offering the sacrifice instead of waiting for Samuel? Is this understandable? Excusable? Why?

_____

_____

_____

4) How is Jonathan compared with his father Saul? How was Jonathan able to win such a victory against the Philistines?

_____

_____

_____

5) How would you describe Saul's final confrontation with Samuel? What excuses did Saul give in this instance for his partial obedience?

_____

_____

Cross-Reference

Consider the New Testament standards for those who would lead God's people.

1 Timothy 3:1–13

¹ *This [is] a faithful saying: If a man desires the position of a bishop, he desires a good work.*

² *A bishop then must be blameless, the husband of one wife, temperate, sober-minded, of good behavior, hospitable, able to teach;*

³ *not given to wine, not violent, not greedy for money, but gentle, not quarrelsome, not covetous;*

⁴ *one who rules his own house well, having [his] children in submission with all reverence*

⁵ *(for if a man does not know how to rule his own house, how will he take care of the church of God?);*

⁶ *not a novice, lest being puffed up with pride he fall into the [same] condemnation as the devil.*

⁷ *Moreover he must have a good testimony among those who are outside, lest he fall into reproach and the snare of the devil.*

⁸ *Likewise deacons [must be] reverent, not double-tongued, not given to much wine, not greedy for money,*

⁹ *holding the mystery of the faith with a pure conscience.*

¹⁰ *But let these also first be tested; then let them serve as deacons, being [found] blameless.*

¹¹ *Likewise [their] wives [must be] reverent, not slanderers, temperate, faithful in all things.*

¹² *Let deacons be the husbands of one wife, ruling [their] children and their own houses well.*

¹³ *For those who have served well as deacons obtain for themselves a good standing and great boldness in the faith which is in Christ Jesus.*

Exploring the Meaning

6) How would you respond to the oft-repeated claim that "nobody could possibly live up to such a rigorous standard"? Why would these also be good qualifications for a political leader?

_____

_____

7) What do these passages reveal about the character of God? Why doesn't our generation have such an awe and respect for God?

_____

_____

8) How would you answer the person who accuses God (and His human spokesman, Samuel) of being harsh or even unmerciful in dealing with the Amalekites?

_____

_____

Summing Up . . .

"The Amalekites make an apt illustration of the sin that remains in the believer's life. That sin—already utterly defeated—must be dealt with ruthlessly and hacked to pieces, or it will revive and continue to plunder and pillage our hearts and sap our spiritual strength. We cannot be merciful to Agag, or he will turn and try to devour us. In fact, the remaining sin in us often becomes more fiercely determined after it has been overthrown by the gospel. . . .

"We cannot obey partially or halfheartedly as we seek to eliminate sin from our lives. We cannot stop while the task remains incomplete. Sins, like Amalekites, have a way of escaping the slaughter, breeding, reviving, regrouping, and launching new and unexpected assaults on our most vulnerable areas." —John MacArthur

Reflecting on the Text

9) Jerry Bridges in his book *The Pursuit of Holiness* argues that most Christians don't make it their goal not to sin; rather, they make it their goal not to sin *too much*. Is this true? How much do you tolerate sin in your own life right now?

_____

_____

10) If you were tapped for a position of leadership and you came under public scrutiny, what actions, attitudes, or habits would you be ashamed for people to find out about you? What does this indicate you need to do?

_____

_____

11) God has certainly not called anyone to hack someone to pieces because of the person's sin, but we *are* called to speak the truth in love in order to turn sinners back from their evil ways. Whom has God put in your life who needs a strong dose of tough love and blunt truth?

How can you be the compassionate and yet courageous voice of God to that person this week?

_____

_____

Recording Your Thoughts

Kim - brain tumor | Ginger - Breast; Mom's Depression (Martha) | Curt's Job sit.

Church Meeting | Eric - health problems wisdom | Regie's Mom, Mothers cousin lost finger

For further study, see the following passages:

Exodus 28:5–13	Leviticus 17:10–14	Judges 6:3–5, 36–40
1 Samuel 17:55, 58	1 Samuel 28:6	2 Samuel 23:8–39
1 Chronicles 22:3	Psalm 51:16	Micah 1:15
Micah 6:6–8	Acts 13:21–22	

David's Rise to Power

1 Samuel 16:1—18:9

Opening Thought

1) Check out this list of actual predictions that proved to be astonishingly bad:

"Drill for oil? You mean drill into the ground to try and find oil? You're crazy."
> Drillers who Edwin L. Drake tried to enlist to his project to drill for oil in 1859.

"Stocks have reached what looks like a permanently high plateau."
> Irving Fisher, Professor of Economics, Yale University, 1929.

"Everything that can be invented has been invented."
> Charles H. Duell, Commissioner, U.S. Office of Patents, 1899.

"Louis Pasteur's theory of germs is ridiculous fiction."
> Pierre Pachet, Professor of Physiology at Toulouse, 1872

"I think there is a world market for maybe five computers."
> Thomas Watson, chairman of IBM, 1943

"Who . . . wants to hear actors talk?"
> H.M. Warner, Warner Brothers, 1927

"We don't like their sound, and guitar music is on the way out."
> Decca Recording Co. rejecting the Beatles, 1962

"Heavier-than-air flying machines are impossible."
> Lord Kelvin, president, Royal Society, 1895

What changes in your life would you never have predicted?

_____

_____

_____

Background of the Passage

Israel's first experience with a monarchical government failed miserably. Saul repeatedly made foolish choices, fearing the people more than God, seeking his own will more than the Lord's. So now, the rejection of the king after the people's heart was followed by the selection of the king after God's own heart.

Here David is introduced. Who ever would have predicted him as God's choice? A shepherd boy. The sweet psalmist of Israel. Small in stature. The youngest brother of an insignificant family. But God directs Samuel to anoint this passionate boy as Israel's next king.

In time David begins serving faithfully in the court of Saul (16:14–23). And in time he proves himself to be a warrior of the Lord (17:1–58). David stands up to the dreaded Philistine Goliath and bravely conquers him. Who ever could have predicted such a feat?

As David's popularity rises, Saul sinks into a whirlpool of paranoia, suspicion, and depression. Yet Saul's own son, Jonathan, heir to the throne, becomes David's closest friend—another unlikely turn in this unpredictable but thrilling period of Israel's history.

Bible Passage

Read 16:1—18:9, noting the key words and definitions to the right of the passage.

1 Samuel 16:1—18:9

¹ Now the LORD said to Samuel, "How long will you mourn for Saul, seeing I have rejected him from reigning over Israel? Fill your horn with oil, and go; I am sending you to Jesse the Bethlehemite. For I have provided Myself a king among his sons."

² And Samuel said, "How can I go? If Saul hears [it], he will kill me." And the LORD said, "Take a heifer with you, and say, 'I have come to sacrifice to the LORD.'

³ "Then invite Jesse to the sacrifice, and I will show you what you shall do; you shall anoint for Me the one I name to you."

⁴ So Samuel did what the LORD said, and went to

Jesse the Bethlehemite (v. 1)—God's new king of Israel (and ultimately the Messiah) would come from Bethlehem of the tribe of Judah.

Saul . . . will kill me (v. 2)—The king's unbalanced state was already evident.

anoint (v. 3)—the first of three; this one was private, the succeeding ones public

Do you come peaceably? (v. 4)—an understandable

Bethlehem. And the elders of the town trembled at his coming, and said, "Do you come peaceably?"

5 And he said, "Peaceably; I have come to sacrifice to the LORD. Sanctify yourselves, and come with me to the sacrifice." Then he consecrated Jesse and his sons, and invited them to the sacrifice.

6 So it was, when they came, that he looked at Eliab and said, "Surely the LORD's anointed [is] before Him."

7 But the LORD said to Samuel, "Do not look at his appearance or at the height of his stature, because I have refused him. For [the LORD does] not [see] as man sees; for man looks at the outward appearance, but the LORD looks at the heart."

8 So Jesse called Abinadab, and made him pass before Samuel. And he said, "Neither has the LORD chosen this one."

9 Then Jesse made Shammah pass by. And he said, "Neither has the LORD chosen this one."

10 Thus Jesse made seven of his sons pass before Samuel. And Samuel said to Jesse, "The LORD has not chosen these."

11 And Samuel said to Jesse, "Are all the young men here?" Then he said, "There remains yet the youngest, and there he is, keeping the sheep." And Samuel said to Jesse, "Send and bring him. For we will not sit down till he comes here."

12 So he sent and brought him in. Now he [was] ruddy, with bright eyes, and good-looking. And the LORD said, "Arise, anoint him; for this [is] the one!"

13 Then Samuel took the horn of oil and anointed him in the midst of his brothers; and the Spirit of the LORD came upon David from that day forward. So Samuel arose and went to Ramah.

14 But the Spirit of the LORD departed from Saul, and a distressing spirit from the LORD troubled him.

15 And Saul's servants said to him, "Surely, a distressing spirit from God is troubling you.

16 "Let our master now command your servants, [who are] before you, to seek out a man [who is] a skillful player on the harp; and it shall be that he will play it with his hand when the distressing spirit from God is upon you, and you shall be well."

17 So Saul said to his servants, "Provide me now a man who can play well, and bring [him] to me."

question in light of Saul's recent execution of Agag

Eliab (v. 6)—the eldest son of Jesse, likely very impressive in appearance

the Lord looks at the heart (v. 7)—God values internal character more than external characteristics.

ruddy . . . bright eyes . . . good-looking (v. 12)—These qualities were not the reason for David's selection but were in addition to his heart for God.

the Spirit of the Lord came upon David (v. 13)—not in a regenerative sense, but rather empowering him for the task ahead

a distressing spirit . . . troubled him (v. 14)—God sovereignly allowed an evil spirit to torment Saul, resulting in severe bouts of depression, anger, and delusion.

¹⁸ *Then one of the servants answered and said, "Look, I have seen a son of Jesse the Bethlehemite, [who is] skillful in playing, a mighty man of valor, a man of war, prudent in speech, and a handsome person; and the LORD [is] with him."*

¹⁹ *Therefore Saul sent messengers to Jesse, and said, "Send me your son David, who [is] with the sheep."*

²⁰ *And Jesse took a donkey [loaded with] bread, a skin of wine, and a young goat, and sent [them] by his son David to Saul.*

²¹ *So David came to Saul and stood before him. And he loved him greatly, and he became his armor-bearer.*

²² *Then Saul sent to Jesse, saying, "Please let David stand before me, for he has found favor in my sight."*

²³ *And so it was, whenever the spirit from God was upon Saul, that David would take a harp and play [it] with his hand. Then Saul would become refreshed and well, and the distressing spirit would depart from him.*

¹ *Now the Philistines gathered their armies together to battle, and were gathered together at Sochoh, which [belongs] to Judah; they encamped between Sochoh and Azekah, in Ephes Dammim.*

² *And Saul and the men of Israel were gathered together, and they encamped in the Valley of Elah, and drew up in battle array against the Philistines.*

³ *The Philistines stood on a mountain on one side, and Israel stood on a mountain on the other side, with a valley between them.*

⁴ *And a champion went out from the camp of the Philistines, named Goliath, from Gath, whose height [was] six cubits and a span.*

⁵ *[He had] a bronze helmet on his head, and he [was] armed with a coat of mail, and the weight of the coat [was] five thousand shekels of bronze.*

⁶ *And [he had] bronze armor on his legs and a bronze javelin between his shoulders.*

⁷ *Now the staff of his spear [was] like a weaver's beam, and his iron spearhead [weighed] six hundred shekels; and a shield-bearer went before him.*

⁸ *Then he stood and cried out to the armies of Israel, and said to them, "Why have you come out to line up for battle? [Am] I not a Philistine, and you the*

skillful in playing (v. 18)—God used David's exceptional musical gifts to introduce him into Saul's court and to soothe Saul's bouts with depression.

he loved him greatly (v. 21)—Saul appreciated David's abilities but eventually would grow to hate the young man.

champion (17:4)—literally "a man between two," an appropriate title for Goliath since he stood between the two armies, challenging Israel's best warrior to a duel

six cubits and a span (v. 4)—A "cubit" measures eighteen inches and a "span" about nine, making Goliath about nine feet nine inches tall!

servants of Saul? Choose a man for yourselves, and let him come down to me.

9 "If he is able to fight with me and kill me, then we will be your servants. But if I prevail against him and kill him, then you shall be our servants and serve us."

10 And the Philistine said, "I defy the armies of Israel this day; give me a man, that we may fight together."

11 When Saul and all Israel heard these words of the Philistine, they were dismayed and greatly afraid.

12 Now David [was] the son of that Ephrathite of Bethlehem Judah, whose name [was] Jesse, and who had eight sons. And the man was old, advanced [in years], in the days of Saul.

13 The three oldest sons of Jesse had gone to follow Saul to the battle. The names of his three sons who went to the battle [were] Eliab the firstborn, next to him Abinadab, and the third Shammah.

14 David [was] the youngest. And the three oldest followed Saul.

15 But David occasionally went and returned from Saul to feed his father's sheep at Bethlehem.

16 And the Philistine drew near and presented himself forty days, morning and evening.

17 Then Jesse said to his son David, "Take now for your brothers an ephah of this dried [grain] and these ten loaves, and run to your brothers at the camp.

18 "And carry these ten cheeses to the captain of [their] thousand, and see how your brothers fare, and bring back news of them."

19 Now Saul and they and all the men of Israel [were] in the Valley of Elah, fighting with the Philistines.

20 So David rose early in the morning, left the sheep with a keeper, and took [the things] and went as Jesse had commanded him. And he came to the camp as the army was going out to the fight and shouting for the battle.

21 For Israel and the Philistines had drawn up in battle array, army against army.

22 And David left his supplies in the hand of the supply keeper, ran to the army, and came and greeted his brothers.

23 Then as he talked with them, there was the champion, the Philistine of Gath, Goliath by name,

David occasionally went and returned from Saul (v. 15)—David's duties were divided between his billet with Saul as one of many armor-bearers (16:21) and tending his father's sheep in Bethlehem.

the same words (v. 23)—the same challenge he'd been making for forty days and nights

coming up from the armies of the Philistines; and he spoke according to the same words. So David heard [them].

24 And all the men of Israel, when they saw the man, fled from him and were dreadfully afraid.

25 So the men of Israel said, "Have you seen this man who has come up? Surely he has come up to defy Israel; and it shall be [that] the man who kills him the king will enrich with great riches, will give him his daughter, and give his father's house exemption [from taxes] in Israel."

26 Then David spoke to the men who stood by him, saying, "What shall be done for the man who kills this Philistine and takes away the reproach from Israel? For who [is] this uncircumcised Philistine, that he should defy the armies of the living God?"

27 And the people answered him in this manner, saying, "So shall it be done for the man who kills him."

28 Now Eliab his oldest brother heard when he spoke to the men; and Eliab's anger was aroused against David, and he said, "Why did you come down here? And with whom have you left those few sheep in the wilderness? I know your pride and the insolence of your heart, for you have come down to see the battle."

29 And David said, "What have I done now? [Is there] not a cause?"

30 Then he turned from him toward another and said the same thing; and these people answered him as the first ones [did].

31 Now when the words which David spoke were heard, they reported [them] to Saul; and he sent for him.

32 Then David said to Saul, "Let no man's heart fail because of him; your servant will go and fight with this Philistine."

33 And Saul said to David, "You are not able to go against this Philistine to fight with him; for you [are] a youth, and he a man of war from his youth."

34 But David said to Saul, "Your servant used to keep his father's sheep, and when a lion or a bear came and took a lamb out of the flock,

35 I went out after it and struck it, and delivered [the lamb] from its mouth; and when it arose against

Eliab's anger (v. 28)—Perhaps Eliab was angry because he was still stinging from being passed over for the kingship of Israel in favor of his younger brother.

You are not able (v. 33)—Saul was not taking into account the presence and power of God in the young man's life.

me, I caught [it] by its beard, and struck and killed it.

36 "Your servant has killed both lion and bear; and this uncircumcised Philistine will be like one of them, seeing he has defied the armies of the living God."

37 Moreover David said, "The LORD, who delivered me from the paw of the lion and from the paw of the bear, He will deliver me from the hand of this Philistine." And Saul said to David, "Go, and the LORD be with you!"

38 So Saul clothed David with his armor, and he put a bronze helmet on his head; he also clothed him with a coat of mail.

39 David fastened his sword to his armor and tried to walk, for he had not tested [them]. And David said to Saul, "I cannot walk with these, for I have not tested [them]." So David took them off.

40 Then he took his staff in his hand; and he chose for himself five smooth stones from the brook, and put them in a shepherd's bag, in a pouch which he had, and his sling was in his hand. And he drew near to the Philistine.

41 So the Philistine came, and began drawing near to David, and the man who bore the shield [went] before him.

42 And when the Philistine looked about and saw David, he disdained him; for he was [only] a youth, ruddy and good-looking.

43 So the Philistine said to David, "[Am] I a dog, that you come to me with sticks?" And the Philistine cursed David by his gods.

44 And the Philistine said to David, "Come to me, and I will give your flesh to the birds of the air and the beasts of the field!"

45 Then David said to the Philistine, "You come to me with a sword, with a spear, and with a javelin. But I come to you in the name of the LORD of hosts, the God of the armies of Israel, whom you have defied.

46 "This day the LORD will deliver you into my hand, and I will strike you and take your head from you. And this day I will give the carcasses of the camp of the Philistines to the birds of the air and the wild beasts of the earth, that all the earth may know that there is a God in Israel.

47 "Then all this assembly shall know that the LORD

The Lord . . . He will deliver me (v. 37)—David's faith in the Lord was wholehearted.

staff . . . stones . . . sling (v. 40)—The tools of the shepherd proved also to be appropriate weapons for Israel's shepherd.

all the earth may know (v. 46)—David fought in the name of the Lord and for the glory of the Lord.

does not save with sword and spear; for the battle [is] the Lord's, and He will give you into our hands."

48 So it was, when the Philistine arose and came and drew near to meet David, that David hastened and ran toward the army to meet the Philistine.

49 Then David put his hand in his bag and took out a stone; and he slung [it] and struck the Philistine in his forehead, so that the stone sank into his forehead, and he fell on his face to the earth.

50 So David prevailed over the Philistine with a sling and a stone, and struck the Philistine and killed him. But [there was] no sword in the hand of David.

51 Therefore David ran and stood over the Philistine, took his sword and drew it out of its sheath and killed him, and cut off his head with it. And when the Philistines saw that their champion was dead, they fled.

52 Now the men of Israel and Judah arose and shouted, and pursued the Philistines as far as the entrance of the valley and to the gates of Ekron. And the wounded of the Philistines fell along the road to Shaaraim, even as far as Gath and Ekron.

53 Then the children of Israel returned from chasing the Philistines, and they plundered their tents.

54 And David took the head of the Philistine and brought it to Jerusalem, but he put his armor in his tent.

55 When Saul saw David going out against the Philistine, he said to Abner, the commander of the army, "Abner, whose son [is] this youth?" And Abner said, "As your soul lives, O king, I do not know."

56 So the king said, "Inquire whose son this young man [is]."

57 Then, as David returned from the slaughter of the Philistine, Abner took him and brought him before Saul with the head of the Philistine in his hand.

58 And Saul said to him, "Whose son [are] you, young man?" So David answered, "[I am] the son of your servant Jesse the Bethlehemite."

1 Now when he had finished speaking to Saul, the soul of Jonathan was knit to the soul of David, and Jonathan loved him as his own soul.

David . . . ran (v. 48)— Unencumbered by armor and emboldened by faith, David rushed into battle.

² *Saul took him that day, and would not let him go home to his father's house anymore.*

³ *Then Jonathan and David made a covenant, because he loved him as his own soul.*

⁴ *And Jonathan took off the robe that [was] on him and gave it to David, with his armor, even to his sword and his bow and his belt.*

⁵ *So David went out wherever Saul sent him, [and] behaved wisely. And Saul set him over the men of war, and he was accepted in the sight of all the people and also in the sight of Saul's servants.*

⁶ *Now it had happened as they were coming [home], when David was returning from the slaughter of the Philistine, that the women had come out of all the cities of Israel, singing and dancing, to meet King Saul, with tambourines, with joy, and with musical instruments.*

⁷ *So the women sang as they danced, and said: "Saul has slain his thousands, And David his ten thousands."*

⁸ *Then Saul was very angry, and the saying displeased him; and he said, "They have ascribed to David ten thousands, and to me they have ascribed [only] thousands. Now [what] more can he have but the kingdom?"*

⁹ *So Saul eyed David from that day forward.*

Jonathan loved him (18:1)—a relationship of covenant love, marked by devotion and loyalty

robe . . . belt (v. 4)—items signifying Jonathan's position as prince of Israel and heir to the throne; by giving them to David he was humbly recognizing David as the Lord's anointed

the kingdom (v. 8)—Saul's jealousy and paranoia began to grow as David's popularity increased.

Understanding the Text

2) For what was Samuel looking in a prospective king for Israel? What lessons did God teach him?

_____

_____

_____

3) These chapters introduce the reader to David as a young man and reveal a number of important details about this future king. What qualities and talents are ascribed to him here that might account for his later successes?

_____

_____

4) How is Saul's descent described in these chapters?

_____

_____

_____

Cross-Reference

Compare this psalm of David to what you have just read.

Psalm 27
¹ *A Psalm of David. The* LORD *[is] my light and my salvation; Whom shall I fear? The* LORD *[is] the strength of my life; Of whom shall I be afraid?*
² *When the wicked came against me To eat up my flesh, My enemies and foes, They stumbled and fell.*
³ *Though an army may encamp against me, My heart shall not fear; Though war should rise against me, In this I [will be] confident.*
⁴ *One [thing] I have desired of the* LORD, *That will I seek: That I may dwell in the house of the* LORD *All the days of my life, To behold the beauty of the* LORD, *And to inquire in His temple.*
⁵ *For in the time of trouble He shall hide me in His pavilion; In the secret place of His tabernacle He shall hide me; He shall set me high upon a rock.*
⁶ *And now my head shall be lifted up above my enemies all around me; Therefore I will offer sacrifices of joy in His tabernacle; I will sing, yes, I will sing praises to the* LORD.
⁷ *Hear, O* LORD, *[when] I cry with my voice! Have mercy also upon me, and answer me.*
⁸ *[When You said], "Seek My face," My heart said to You, "Your face,* LORD, *I will seek."*
⁹ *Do not hide Your face from me; Do not turn Your servant away in anger; You have been my help; Do not leave me nor forsake me, O God of my salvation.*
¹⁰ *When my father and my mother forsake me, Then the* LORD *will take care of me.*
¹¹ *Teach me Your way, O* LORD, *And lead me in a smooth path, because of my enemies.*
¹² *Do not deliver me to the will of my adversaries; For false witnesses have risen against me, And such as breathe out violence.*
¹³ *[I would have lost heart], unless I had believed That I would see the goodness of the* LORD *In the land of the living.*
¹⁴ *Wait on the* LORD; *Be of good courage, And He shall strengthen your heart; Wait, I say, on the* LORD!

Exploring the Meaning

5) What does this psalm reveal about David's faith? What insight does it provide into David's spiritual character and state of mind as he prepared to face Goliath?

_____

_____

_____

6) What is significant about the fact that when the Spirit of the Lord departed from Saul, an evil spirit was allowed by God to torment the king?

_____

_____

_____

(verses to consider: Matthew 12:43–45; 1 Corinthians 5:1–7; Ephesians 4:27; 1 Timothy 4:1; 1 John 4:1–4)

Summing Up . . .

"God took the kingdom from Saul because he refused to live by the new heart God had given him. He gave the kingdom to David because David was 'a man after [God's] own heart' (13:14). David pleased God's heart because God pleased David's heart. 'I will praise You, O Lord, with my whole heart,' he sang (Psalm 9:1). His deepest desire was, 'Let the words of my mouth and the meditation of my heart be acceptable in Your sight, O Lord, my strength and my Redeemer' (Psalm 19:14). He prayed, 'Examine me, O Lord, and prove me; try my mind and my heart' (Psalm 26:2). When God told David, 'Seek my face,' David's heart replied, 'Your face, Lord, I will seek' (Psalm 27:8). . . . David often failed, but his heart was fixed on God." —_John MacArthur_

Reflecting on the Text

8) As we look more closely at David's life, it is _not_ surprising that God would choose him to be Israel's king. Why do we so often take such a superficial,

shallow view of people and events? How can you begin to look beneath the surface this week and see as God sees?

_____

_____

9) What kind of Goliath-sized problem are you facing? What does the example of David tell you that you need to do in order to face and defeat this giant?

_____

_____

_____

10) Taking a cue from Jonathan and David, what is something specific and practical you can do this week to build a deeper (or even a new and unexpected) friendship?

_____

_____

_____

Recording Your Thoughts

Kathryn + Tom / Ginger leading small group leaders / Becca
Corey - J.O.B / Jennifer J.OB / Chill Ben
Stephen's uncle/cousins

For further study, see the following passages:

Genesis 49:10	Exodus 19:10	Numbers 13:30
Numbers 24:17	Deuteronomy 12:11	Deuteronomy 20:1–5
Joshua 4:24	Joshua 15:13–17	Judges 7:18
Judges 9:23	1 Samuel 2:10	1 Samuel 18:29
2 Samuel 2:7	2 Samuel 5:11	2 Samuel 23:1
2 Chronicles 20:14	Job 1:6–12	Psalm 51:11
Psalm 89:27	Matthew 12:34–35	

Saul's Jealousy

1 Samuel 18:10—20:42

Opening Thought

1) What's the biggest trial you've ever faced? What eventually happened?

_____

_____

2) What's the closest you've ever come to dying? How did that event affect you? How did it alter your walk with God?

_____

_____

3) What's the longest you've ever had to wait for something? What was that experience like?

_____

_____

?a demonstrate David's position as anointed but not yet king

Background of the Passage

Saul's kingship had been a disaster, and consequently he was rejected in favor of the godly David. In the perfect, sovereign plan of God, however, the transition has not yet taken place. In fact, it is still years away. Why?

The Lord's ways are not our ways. Apparently the principal characters in this political and theological drama still had lessons to learn and principles to teach. God made the lives of Saul and David not

73

only for His glory, but also to be powerful object lessons both for their contemporaries and for all who would follow.

David's slow rise to power was not without its obstacles and trials. In contrast to Jonathan's love and faithful friendship, David faced the growing anger and demonic jealousy of King Saul (18:11–30). Saul's paranoia reached the level that he even tried to convince Jonathan to kill the popular David, his closest friend. Failing in this, Saul himself tried to pin David to the wall with a javelin!

The hand of God was on the future king. David escaped and continued to elude Saul with the help of Saul's own children, son Jonathan, and daughter Michal, who had become David's wife.

God never promised that following Him would be easy.

Bible Passage

Read 18:10—20:42, noting the key words and definitions to the right of the passage.

1 Samuel 18:10—20:42

¹⁰ And it happened on the next day that the distressing spirit from God came upon Saul, and he prophesied inside the house. So David played [music] with his hand, as at other times; but [there was] a spear in Saul's hand.

¹¹ And Saul cast the spear, for he said, "I will pin David to the wall!" But David escaped his presence twice.

¹² Now Saul was afraid of David, because the LORD was with him, but had departed from Saul.

¹³ Therefore Saul removed him from his presence, and made him his captain over a thousand; and he went out and came in before the people.

¹⁴ And David behaved wisely in all his ways, and the LORD [was] with him.

¹⁵ Therefore, when Saul saw that he behaved very wisely, he was afraid of him.

¹⁶ But all Israel and Judah loved David, because he went out and came in before them.

¹⁷ Then Saul said to David, "Here is my older daughter Merab; I will give her to you as a wife. Only be

the distressing spirit (v. 10)—This spirit tormented Saul into his painful descent.

David escaped . . . twice (v. 11)—Saul's murderous urges were frequent; that David was not hurt by these attempts at the hand of an experienced warrior is proof of God's hand on his life.

Saul was afraid (v. 12)—In his paranoia, Saul saw David as a threat rather than a blessing to Israel.

all Israel and Judah loved David (v. 16)—Saul's attempt to give David a military commission and send him into a kind of honorable exile only showcased David's ability and created even more popularity for the king-in-waiting.

valiant for me, and fight the LORD's battles." For Saul thought, "Let my hand not be against him, but let the hand of the Philistines be against him."

18 *So David said to Saul, "Who [am] I, and what [is] my life [or] my father's family in Israel, that I should be son-in-law to the king?"*

19 *But it happened at the time when Merab, Saul's daughter, should have been given to David, that she was given to Adriel the Meholathite as a wife.*

20 *Now Michal, Saul's daughter, loved David. And they told Saul, and the thing pleased him.*

21 *So Saul said, "I will give her to him, that she may be a snare to him, and that the hand of the Philistines may be against him." Therefore Saul said to David a second time, "You shall be my son-in-law today."*

22 *And Saul commanded his servants, "Communicate with David secretly, and say, 'Look, the king has delight in you, and all his servants love you. Now therefore, become the king's son-in-law.'"*

23 *So Saul's servants spoke those words in the hearing of David. And David said, "Does it seem to you [a] light [thing] to be a king's son-in-law, seeing I [am] a poor and lightly esteemed man?"*

24 *And the servants of Saul told him, saying, "In this manner David spoke."*

25 *Then Saul said, "Thus you shall say to David: 'The king does not desire any dowry but one hundred foreskins of the Philistines, to take vengeance on the king's enemies.'" But Saul thought to make David fall by the hand of the Philistines.*

26 *So when his servants told David these words, it pleased David well to become the king's son-in-law. Now the days had not expired;*

27 *therefore David arose and went, he and his men, and killed two hundred men of the Philistines. And David brought their foreskins, and they gave them in full count to the king, that he might become the king's son-in-law. Then Saul gave him Michal his daughter as a wife.*

28 *Thus Saul saw and knew that the LORD [was] with David, and [that] Michal, Saul's daughter, loved him;*

29 *and Saul was still more afraid of David. So Saul became David's enemy continually.*

30 *Then the princes of the Philistines went out [to*

Merab (v. 17)—Saul later reneged on this offer.

Philistines (vv. 17, 21)—Saul hoped that the Philistines might destroy David in battle.

Michal (v. 20)—the daughter of Saul who loved David and whom the king, with sinister motives, offered to him as a wife

foreskins (vv. 25, 27)—Such mutilation of the slain bodies of enemies was common in ancient warfare.

Saul became David's enemy (v. 29)—Since none of his secret ploys had worked, Saul declared open "war" on his servant David.

war]. And so it was, whenever they went out, [that] David behaved more wisely than all the servants of Saul, so that his name became highly esteemed.

1 *Now Saul spoke to Jonathan his son and to all his servants, that they should kill David;*
2 *but Jonathan, Saul's son, delighted greatly in David. So Jonathan told David, saying, "My father Saul seeks to kill you. Therefore please be on your guard until morning, and stay in a secret [place] and hide.*
3 *"And I will go out and stand beside my father in the field where you [are], and I will speak with my father about you. Then what I observe, I will tell you."*
4 *Thus Jonathan spoke well of David to Saul his father, and said to him, "Let not the king sin against his servant, against David, because he has not sinned against you, and because his works [have been] very good toward you.*
5 *"For he took his life in his hands and killed the Philistine, and the LORD brought about a great deliverance for all Israel. You saw [it] and rejoiced. Why then will you sin against innocent blood, to kill David without a cause?"*
6 *So Saul heeded the voice of Jonathan, and Saul swore, "[As] the LORD lives, he shall not be killed."*
7 *Then Jonathan called David, and Jonathan told him all these things. So Jonathan brought David to Saul, and he was in his presence as in times past.*
8 *And there was war again; and David went out and fought with the Philistines, and struck them with a mighty blow, and they fled from him.*
9 *Now the distressing spirit from the LORD came upon Saul as he sat in his house with his spear in his hand. And David was playing [music] with [his] hand.*
10 *Then Saul sought to pin David to the wall with the spear, but he slipped away from Saul's presence; and he drove the spear into the wall. So David fled and escaped that night.*
11 *Saul also sent messengers to David's house to watch him and to kill him in the morning. And Michal, David's wife, told him, saying, "If you do not save your life tonight, tomorrow you will be killed."*

Jonathan spoke well of David (19:4)—The king's son served as David's faithful and persuasive advocate in Saul's court.

he shall not be killed (v. 6)—Saul listened, but only temporarily, to Jonathan's reasonable arguments.

Michal . . . told him (v. 11)—Rather than being a snare to David, Michal helped save his life.

¹² So Michal let David down through a window. And he went and fled and escaped.

¹³ And Michal took an image and laid [it] in the bed, put a cover of goats' [hair] for his head, and covered [it] with clothes.

¹⁴ So when Saul sent messengers to take David, she said, "He [is] sick."

¹⁵ Then Saul sent the messengers [back] to see David, saying, "Bring him up to me in the bed, that I may kill him."

¹⁶ And when the messengers had come in, there was the image in the bed, with a cover of goats' [hair] for his head.

¹⁷ Then Saul said to Michal, "Why have you deceived me like this, and sent my enemy away, so that he has escaped?" And Michal answered Saul, "He said to me, 'Let me go! Why should I kill you?'"

¹⁸ So David fled and escaped, and went to Samuel at Ramah, and told him all that Saul had done to him. And he and Samuel went and stayed in Naioth.

¹⁹ Now it was told Saul, saying, "Take note, David [is] at Naioth in Ramah!"

²⁰ Then Saul sent messengers to take David. And when they saw the group of prophets prophesying, and Samuel standing [as] leader over them, the Spirit of God came upon the messengers of Saul, and they also prophesied.

²¹ And when Saul was told, he sent other messengers, and they prophesied likewise. Then Saul sent messengers again the third time, and they prophesied also.

²² Then he also went to Ramah, and came to the great well that [is] at Sechu. So he asked, and said, "Where [are] Samuel and David?" And [someone] said, "Indeed [they are] at Naioth in Ramah."

²³ So he went there to Naioth in Ramah. Then the Spirit of God was upon him also, and he went on and prophesied until he came to Naioth in Ramah.

²⁴ And he also stripped off his clothes and prophesied before Samuel in like manner, and lay down naked all that day and all that night. Therefore they say, "[Is] Saul also among the prophets?"

¹ Then David fled from Naioth in Ramah, and went and said to Jonathan, "What have I done? What

an image (v. 13)—a kind of idol or household god, large enough to give the appearance of a sleeping man

the group of prophets prophesying (v. 20)—Saul's messengers were swayed from the task of capturing David by this band of godly men who were speaking the Word of the Lord; they even joined them.

he . . . prophesied before Samuel (v. 24)—God intervened and saved David's life by sending His Spirit upon Saul one last time; the king took off his royal garments (symbolic of his rejection by God) and prophesied.

[is] my iniquity, and what [is] my sin before your father, that he seeks my life?"

2 So Jonathan said to him, "By no means! You shall not die! Indeed, my father will do nothing either great or small without first telling me. And why should my father hide this thing from me? It [is] not [so]!"

3 Then David took an oath again, and said, "Your father certainly knows that I have found favor in your eyes, and he has said, 'Do not let Jonathan know this, lest he be grieved.' But truly, [as] the LORD lives and [as] your soul lives, [there is] but a step between me and death."

4 So Jonathan said to David, "Whatever you yourself desire, I will do [it] for you."

5 And David said to Jonathan, "Indeed tomorrow [is] the New Moon, and I should not fail to sit with the king to eat. But let me go, that I may hide in the field until the third [day] at evening.

6 "If your father misses me at all, then say, 'David earnestly asked [permission] of me that he might run over to Bethlehem, his city, for [there is] a yearly sacrifice there for all the family.'

7 "If he says thus: '[It is] well,' your servant will be safe. But if he is very angry, [then] be sure that evil is determined by him.

8 "Therefore you shall deal kindly with your servant, for you have brought your servant into a covenant of the LORD with you. Nevertheless, if there is iniquity in me, kill me yourself, for why should you bring me to your father?"

9 But Jonathan said, "Far be it from you! For if I knew certainly that evil was determined by my father to come upon you, then would I not tell you?"

10 Then David said to Jonathan, "Who will tell me, or what [if] your father answers you roughly?"

11 And Jonathan said to David, "Come, and let us go out into the field." So both of them went out into the field.

12 Then Jonathan said to David: "The LORD God of Israel [is witness]! When I have sounded out my father sometime tomorrow, [or] the third [day], and indeed [there is] good toward David, and I do not send to you and tell you,

13 "may the LORD do so and much more to Jonathan. But if it pleases my father [to do] you evil, then I

will report it to you and send you away, that you may go in safety. And the LORD be with you as He has been with my father.

14 "And you shall not only show me the kindness of the LORD while I still live, that I may not die;

15 "but you shall not cut off your kindness from my house forever, no, not when the LORD has cut off every one of the enemies of David from the face of the earth."

16 So Jonathan made [a covenant] with the house of David, [saying], "Let the LORD require [it] at the hand of David's enemies."

17 Now Jonathan again caused David to vow, because he loved him; for he loved him as he loved his own soul.

18 Then Jonathan said to David, "Tomorrow [is] the New Moon; and you will be missed, because your seat will be empty.

19 "And [when] you have stayed three days, go down quickly and come to the place where you hid on the day of the deed; and remain by the stone Ezel.

20 "Then I will shoot three arrows to the side, as though I shot at a target;

21 "and there I will send a lad, [saying], 'Go, find the arrows.' If I expressly say to him, 'Look, the arrows [are] on this side of you; get them and come'—then, as the LORD lives, [there is] safety for you and no harm.

22 "But if I say thus to the young man, 'Look, the arrows [are] beyond you'—go your way, for the LORD has sent you away.

23 "And as for the matter which you and I have spoken of, indeed the LORD [be] between you and me forever."

24 Then David hid in the field. And when the New Moon had come, the king sat down to eat the feast.

25 Now the king sat on his seat, as at other times, on a seat by the wall. And Jonathan arose, and Abner sat by Saul's side, but David's place was empty.

26 Nevertheless Saul did not say anything that day, for he thought, "Something has happened to him; he [is] unclean, surely he [is] unclean."

27 And it happened the next day, the second [day] of the month, that David's place was empty. And Saul said to Jonathan his son, "Why has the son of Jesse not come to eat, either yesterday or today?"

the kindness of the Lord (v. 14)—Aware that David would one day be king, Jonathan asked for protection for his family.

as his own soul (v. 17)—the kind of sacrificial, other-centered love called for by both the Mosaic Law and Christ

the stone Ezel (v. 19)— obviously a well-known or clearly distinguishable landmark at the time

28 *So Jonathan answered Saul, "David earnestly asked [permission] of me [to go] to Bethlehem.*

29 *"And he said, 'Please let me go, for our family has a sacrifice in the city, and my brother has commanded me [to be there]. And now, if I have found favor in your eyes, please let me get away and see my brothers.' Therefore he has not come to the king's table."*

30 *Then Saul's anger was aroused against Jonathan, and he said to him, "You son of a perverse, rebellious [woman]! Do I not know that you have chosen the son of Jesse to your own shame and to the shame of your mother's nakedness?*

31 *"For as long as the son of Jesse lives on the earth, you shall not be established, nor your kingdom. Now therefore, send and bring him to me, for he shall surely die."*

32 *And Jonathan answered Saul his father, and said to him, "Why should he be killed? What has he done?"*

33 *Then Saul cast a spear at him to kill him, by which Jonathan knew that it was determined by his father to kill David.*

34 *So Jonathan arose from the table in fierce anger, and ate no food the second day of the month, for he was grieved for David, because his father had treated him shamefully.*

35 *And so it was, in the morning, that Jonathan went out into the field at the time appointed with David, and a little lad [was] with him.*

36 *Then he said to his lad, "Now run, find the arrows which I shoot." As the lad ran, he shot an arrow beyond him.*

37 *When the lad had come to the place where the arrow was which Jonathan had shot, Jonathan cried out after the lad and said, "[Is] not the arrow beyond you?"*

38 *And Jonathan cried out after the lad, "Make haste, hurry, do not delay!" So Jonathan's lad gathered up the arrows and came back to his master.*

39 *But the lad did not know anything. Only Jonathan and David knew of the matter.*

40 *Then Jonathan gave his weapons to his lad, and said to him, "Go, carry [them] to the city."*

41 *As soon as the lad had gone, David arose from [a] place toward the south, fell on his face to the*

son of a perverse, rebellious woman (v. 30)—Saul was furious at his own son for siding with his perceived enemy, David.

bowed down three times (v. 41)—an acknowledgment of Jonathan's princely status and an expression of humble affection

ground, and bowed down three times. And they
kissed one another; and they wept together, but
David more so.

42 Then Jonathan said to David, "Go in peace, since
we have both sworn in the name of the LORD, saying, 'May the LORD be between you and me, and
between your descendants and my descendants, forever.'" So he arose and departed, and Jonathan
went into the city.

Understanding the Text

4) How do these chapters depict Saul's deteriorating state of mind?

Multiple (3) attempts to pin David, Once at Jon
Seeks to trick/send David into death,
Plagued by "distressing spirit"

5) In what ways did Saul try to harm or even kill David? Why didn't he succeed?

3x spears, sends out to Philistines, sends
soldiers to kill him at home — God facilitates
escape, either directly, or via Saul's kids

(verses to consider: Acts 5:38–39; 26:14–15)

6) What are some of the means that God used to protect His anointed servant?

Saul's children love & protect David, allowed
David victories - love of people, blessed
w/wisdom, caused messengers to prophesy,
Samuel's protection, thwarts Saul w/ spirit

Cross-Reference

This passage in 1 Samuel is the likely background for Psalm 59.

1 To the Chief Musician. Set to "Do Not Destroy." A Michtam of David when Saul
sent men, and they watched the house in order to kill him. Deliver me from my
enemies, O my God; Defend me from those who rise up against me.

² *Deliver me from the workers of iniquity, And save me from bloodthirsty men.*

³ *For look, they lie in wait for my life; The mighty gather against me, Not [for] my transgression nor [for] my sin, O LORD.*

⁴ *They run and prepare themselves through no fault [of mine]. Awake to help me, and behold!*

⁵ *You therefore, O LORD God of hosts, the God of Israel, Awake to punish all the nations; Do not be merciful to any wicked transgressors. Selah*

⁶ *At evening they return, They growl like a dog, And go all around the city.*

⁷ *Indeed, they belch with their mouth; Swords [are] in their lips; For [they say], "Who hears?"*

⁸ *But You, O LORD, shall laugh at them; You shall have all the nations in derision.*

⁹ *I will wait for You, [O You] his Strength; For God [is] my defense;*

¹⁰ *My God of mercy shall come to meet me; God shall let me see [my desire] on my enemies.*

¹¹ *Do not slay them, lest my people forget; Scatter them by Your power, And bring them down, O LORD our shield.*

¹² *[For] the sin of their mouth [and] the words of their lips, Let them even be taken in their pride, And for the cursing and lying [which] they speak.*

¹³ *Consume [them] in wrath, consume [them], That they [may] not [be]; And let them know that God rules in Jacob To the ends of the earth. Selah*

¹⁴ *And at evening they return, They growl like a dog, And go all around the city.*

¹⁵ *They wander up and down for food, And howl if they are not satisfied.*

¹⁶ *But I will sing of Your power; Yes, I will sing aloud of Your mercy in the morning; For You have been my defense And refuge in the day of my trouble.*

¹⁷ *To You, O my Strength, I will sing praises; For God [is] my defense, My God of mercy.*

Exploring the Meaning

7) What does this psalm reveal about David's enemies (the soldiers of Saul)? About David himself? About God?

Recurring enemies — David more persistent in exercise of faith than are enemies in mission to kill
David looks to God for deliverance — not himself, no scheming

8) What was it like for David to know that He had been chosen to be king, and yet to have to not only wait, but also to dodge (literally) Saul's attempts to take his life?

_____

_____

_____

9) Read 2 Corinthians 11:23–33. What does this passage say about the kinds of trials God's servants will face? About their ultimate security and safety?

Many & varied, but to be boasted of b/c God will prevail regardless — no security in this life, only through salvation

Summing Up . . .

"Worry is not a trivial sin because it strikes a blow both at God's love and at God's integrity. Worry declares our heavenly Father to be untrustworthy in His Word and His promises. To avow belief in the inerrancy of Scripture and in the next moment to express worry is to speak out of both sides of our mouths. Worry shows that we are mastered by our circumstances and by our finite perspectives and understanding rather than by God's Word. Worry is therefore not only debilitating and destructive but maligns and impugns God." —_John MacArthur_

Reflecting on the Text

10) Like David, are you facing severe trials and tempted to doubt God's promise, and yield to anxiety and fear? What specific steps can you take today to combat the tendency to worry and to increase your faith?

Seek allies, pray
Actively scrutinize mindset — are you worrying or resting in faith

_____

_____

11) What people (like Jonathan and Michal) has God put in your life to help you through? Are you utilizing these human gifts? For whom could you be an encouragement today?

_____

_____

_____

_____

12) Write a short psalm-like poem in which you describe a current difficulty and express your trust in God.

_____

_____

_____

_____

Recording Your Thoughts.

Becca - heart stopped, infection

Ginger/Stephen trying to adopt Chinese human baby.

Kathryn - Sister pregnant (christine), husband left.

Jennifer's Job

_____

_____

_____

For further study, see the following passages:

Genesis 29:25	Genesis 31:30–35	Leviticus 19:18
Numbers 11:23	Deuteronomy 21:8–9	Joshua 9:20
2 Samuel 9:1–8	2 Samuel 11:15	2 Samuel 23:8–39
1 Kings 22:19–23	2 Kings 4:23	Matthew 22:39

David in Exile

12/9/04

Opening Thought

1) Fear is one of life's most powerful emotions. Let something threaten our well-being and suddenly our faith is put to the ultimate test.

Rank the following items in terms of how fearful they are to you (1 is "terrifying"; 10 is "no big deal").

_____ having to stand and speak to a large gathering
_____ discovering that you have a terminal disease
_____ becoming paralyzed or handicapped
_____ being called by God to do something very difficult
         (for example, be a missionary overseas)
_____ experiencing financial devastation
_____ dying
_____ failing in your career
_____ losing a loved one
_____ having unbelieving or wayward children
_____ having to face a certain phobia (for example, fear of heights,
         fear of flying, fear of water, etc.)

2) Why do we become so frantic when facing scary situations and so prone to take matters into our own hands rather than trust God?

_____

_____

3) To what sinful temptations might you yield if you were facing your worst fear?

_____

_____

Background of the Passage

Despite the prophet Samuel's warnings, the people of Israel had demanded a king and had been granted one in the person of Saul. Because of repeated disobedience, however, Saul had been rejected by God. In his place, God intended to make David the new king of Israel.

Saul would not relinquish the crown without a struggle, however. No longer possessing the Spirit of God and, in fact, being oppressed by an evil spirit, he quickly became a pathetic figure. Jealous, paranoid, angry, and violent, Saul foolishly attempted to destroy the Lord's anointed.

What would David do? He had done nothing wrong. He had been a faithful servant to both the Lord and Saul. God had promised to make him king, but Saul had pledged to kill him. Would David trust in the Lord? Or would he yield to strong fears and violate his integrity in dangerous situations?

These chapters, though describing events thousands of years ago, are timely in that they provide wonderful lessons and helpful examples (both good and bad) for what to do in uncertain, frightening times.

Bible Passage

Read 21:1—23:29, noting the key words and definitions to the right of the passage.

1 Samuel 21:1—23:29

1 Now David came to Nob, to Ahimelech the priest. And Ahimelech was afraid when he met David, and said to him, "Why [are] you alone, and no one is with you?"
2 So David said to Ahimelech the priest, "The king has ordered me on some business, and said to me, 'Do not let anyone know anything about the business on which I send you, or what I have commanded you.' And I have directed [my] young men to such and such a place.
3 "Now therefore, what have you on hand? Give [me] five [loaves of] bread in my hand, or whatever can be found."
4 And the priest answered David and said, "[There

Ahimelech (21:1)—a great grandson of Eli (1:9); thus a disqualified priest (2:30-36)

The king has ordered me (v. 2)—Out of fear, David lied; he wanted the priest to think he was on official business for the king, an act that resulted in the death of the priests.

is] no common bread on hand; but there is holy bread, if the young men have at least kept themselves from women."

5 *Then David answered the priest, and said to him, "Truly, women [have been] kept from us about three days since I came out. And the vessels of the young men are holy, and [the bread is] in effect common, even though it was sanctified in the vessel this day."*

6 *So the priest gave him holy [bread]; for there was no bread there but the showbread which had been taken from before the LORD, in order to put hot bread [in its place] on the day when it was taken away.*

7 *Now a certain man of the servants of Saul [was] there that day, detained before the LORD. And his name [was] Doeg, an Edomite, the chief of the herdsmen who [belonged] to Saul.*

8 *And David said to Ahimelech, "Is there not here on hand a spear or a sword? For I have brought neither my sword nor my weapons with me, because the king's business required haste."*

9 *So the priest said, "The sword of Goliath the Philistine, whom you killed in the Valley of Elah, there it is, wrapped in a cloth behind the ephod. If you will take that, take [it]. For [there is] no other except that one here." And David said, "[There is] none like it; give it to me."*

10 *Then David arose and fled that day from before Saul, and went to Achish the king of Gath.*

11 *And the servants of Achish said to him, "[Is] this not David the king of the land? Did they not sing of him to one another in dances, saying: 'Saul has slain his thousands, And David his ten thousands'?"*

12 *Now David took these words to heart, and was very much afraid of Achish the king of Gath.*

13 *So he changed his behavior before them, feigned madness in their hands, scratched on the doors of the gate, and let his saliva fall down on his beard.*

14 *Then Achish said to his servants, "Look, you see the man is insane. Why have you brought him to me?*

15 *"Have I need of madmen, that you have brought this [fellow] to play the madman in my presence? Shall this [fellow] come into my house?"*

holy bread (v. 4)—The consecrated bread for use in the tabernacle was to be eaten only by the priests.

kept themselves from women (v. 4)—That is, they were ceremonially clean, though they were not on a spiritual mission (see Exodus 19:15).

vessels (v. 5)—a euphemism for the bodies of the young men

bread . . . common (v. 5–6)—This was bread no longer on the altar, having been replaced by fresh bread on the Sabbath.

Doeg, an Edomite (v. 7)—the head shepherd of Saul's herd, who told Saul about this encounter between David and Ahimelech

the sword of Goliath (v. 9)—kept as a memorial to God's deliverance

Achish the king of Gath (v. 10)—a Philistine king; going here (with the sword of Goliath) was a dangerous decision since David was hated by the Philistines

changed his behavior (v. 13)—David feigned insanity out of fear for his life in hopes that Achish would send him away.

¹ *David therefore departed from there and escaped to the cave of Adullam. And when his brothers and all his father's house heard [it], they went down there to him.*

² *And everyone [who was] in distress, everyone who [was] in debt, and everyone [who was] discontented gathered to him. So he became captain over them. And there were about four hundred men with him.*

³ *Then David went from there to Mizpah of Moab; and he said to the king of Moab, "Please let my father and mother come here with you, till I know what God will do for me."*

⁴ *So he brought them before the king of Moab, and they dwelt with him all the time that David was in the stronghold.*

⁵ *Now the prophet Gad said to David, "Do not stay in the stronghold; depart, and go to the land of Judah." So David departed and went into the forest of Hereth.*

⁶ *When Saul heard that David and the men who [were] with him had been discovered—now Saul was staying in Gibeah under a tamarisk tree in Ramah, with his spear in his hand, and all his servants standing about him—*

⁷ *then Saul said to his servants who stood about him, "Hear now, you Benjamites! Will the son of Jesse give every one of you fields and vineyards, [and] make you all captains of thousands and captains of hundreds?*

⁸ *"All of you have conspired against me, and [there is] no one who reveals to me that my son has made a covenant with the son of Jesse; and [there is] not one of you who is sorry for me or reveals to me that my son has stirred up my servant against me, to lie in wait, as [it is] this day."*

⁹ *Then answered Doeg the Edomite, who was set over the servants of Saul, and said, "I saw the son of Jesse going to Nob, to Ahimelech the son of Ahitub.*

¹⁰ *"And he inquired of the LORD for him, gave him provisions, and gave him the sword of Goliath the Philistine."*

¹¹ *So the king sent to call Ahimelech the priest, the son of Ahitub, and all his father's house, the priests who [were] in Nob. And they all came to the king.*

¹² *And Saul said, "Hear now, son of Ahitub!" And he answered, "Here I am, my lord."*

brothers and all his father's house (22:1)—David's family members went down from Bethlehem, a journey of about twelve miles, to join him at the cave of Adullam.

king of Moab (v. 3)—probably a mutual enemy of Saul, and a potential ally, since David had a Moabitess for a great-grandmother (that is, Ruth)

prophet Gad (v. 5)—Just as Samuel had advised Saul, Gad gave guidance to David.

to lie in wait (vv. 8–13)—Saul accused David of plotting to take his life; actually, David would later spare Saul's life, twice.

13 Then Saul said to him, "Why have you conspired against me, you and the son of Jesse, in that you have given him bread and a sword, and have inquired of God for him, that he should rise against me, to lie in wait, as it is this day?"

14 So Ahimelech answered the king and said, "And who among all your servants [is as] faithful as David, who is the king's son-in-law, who goes at your bidding, and is honorable in your house?

15 "Did I then begin to inquire of God for him? Far be it from me! Let not the king impute anything to his servant, [or] to any in the house of my father. For your servant knew nothing of all this, little or much."

16 And the king said, "You shall surely die, Ahimelech, you and all your father's house!"

17 Then the king said to the guards who stood about him, "Turn and kill the priests of the LORD, because their hand also [is] with David, and because they knew when he fled and did not tell it to me." But the servants of the king would not lift their hands to strike the priests of the LORD.

18 And the king said to Doeg, "You turn and kill the priests!" So Doeg the Edomite turned and struck the priests, and killed on that day eighty-five men who wore a linen ephod.

19 Also Nob, the city of the priests, he struck with the edge of the sword, both men and women, children and nursing infants, oxen and donkeys and sheep— with the edge of the sword.

20 Now one of the sons of Ahimelech the son of Ahitub, named Abiathar, escaped and fled after David.

21 And Abiathar told David that Saul had killed the LORD's priests.

22 So David said to Abiathar, "I knew that day, when Doeg the Edomite [was] there, that he would surely tell Saul. I have caused [the death] of all the persons of your father's house.

23 "Stay with me; do not fear. For he who seeks my life seeks your life, but with me you [shall be] safe."

1 Then they told David, saying, "Look, the Philistines are fighting against Keilah, and they are robbing the threshing floors."

2 Therefore David inquired of the LORD, saying, "Shall I go and attack these Philistines?" And the

your bidding (v. 14)— Ahimelech defended David's character as loyal to Saul.

You shall surely die (v. 16)— a fulfillment of the curse on Eli's house

would not . . . strike the priests (v. 17)—Saul's men refused to raise their weapons against the Lord's priests.

Nob . . . he struck (v. 19)— What Saul refused to do to the wicked Amalekites, he did to the innocent citizens of Nob.

Abiathar (v. 20)—a son of Ahimelech who escaped the slaughter and joined David's band, ministering to him for the rest of his life

I have sinned (v. 22)—David took responsibility for the devastating consequences of his life to Ahimelech.

inquired of the Lord (23:2)— God's will was sought using the sacred stones, the Urim and Thummim, stored in the priestly ephod that Abiathar brought to David.

LORD said to David, "Go and attack the Philistines, and save Keilah."

3 But David's men said to him, "Look, we are afraid here in Judah. How much more then if we go to Keilah against the armies of the Philistines?"

4 Then David inquired of the LORD once again. And the LORD answered him and said, "Arise, go down to Keilah. For I will deliver the Philistines into your hand."

5 And David and his men went to Keilah and fought with the Philistines, struck them with a mighty blow, and took away their livestock. So David saved the inhabitants of Keilah.

6 Now it happened, when Abiathar the son of Ahimelech fled to David at Keilah, [that] he went down [with] an ephod in his hand.

7 And Saul was told that David had gone to Keilah. So Saul said, "God has delivered him into my hand, for he has shut himself in by entering a town that has gates and bars."

8 Then Saul called all the people together for war, to go down to Keilah to besiege David and his men.

9 When David knew that Saul plotted evil against him, he said to Abiathar the priest, "Bring the ephod here."

10 Then David said, "O LORD God of Israel, Your servant has certainly heard that Saul seeks to come to Keilah to destroy the city for my sake.

11 "Will the men of Keilah deliver me into his hand? Will Saul come down, as Your servant has heard? O LORD God of Israel, I pray, tell Your servant." And the LORD said, "He will come down."

12 Then David said, "Will the men of Keilah deliver me and my men into the hand of Saul?" And the LORD said, "They will deliver [you]."

13 So David and his men, about six hundred, arose and departed from Keilah and went wherever they could go. Then it was told Saul that David had escaped from Keilah; so he halted the expedition.

14 And David stayed in strongholds in the wilderness, and remained in the mountains in the Wilderness of Ziph. Saul sought him every day, but God did not deliver him into his hand.

15 So David saw that Saul had come out to seek his life. And David [was] in the Wilderness of Ziph in a forest.

shut himself in (v. 7)—Keilah had, apparently, only one entrance and exit; Saul believed that he had David trapped.

strongholds in the wilderness (v. 14)—a barren desert area with many ravines and caves, perfect for hiding

16 Then Jonathan, Saul's son, arose and went to David in the woods and strengthened his hand in God.

17 And he said to him, "Do not fear, for the hand of Saul my father shall not find you. You shall be king over Israel, and I shall be next to you. Even my father Saul knows that."

18 So the two of them made a covenant before the LORD. And David stayed in the woods, and Jonathan went to his own house.

19 Then the Ziphites came up to Saul at Gibeah, saying, "Is David not hiding with us in strongholds in the woods, in the hill of Hachilah, which [is] on the south of Jeshimon?

20 "Now therefore, O king, come down according to all the desire of your soul to come down; and our part [shall be] to deliver him into the king's hand."

21 And Saul said, "Blessed [are] you of the LORD, for you have compassion on me.

22 "Please go and find out for sure, and see the place where his hideout is, [and] who has seen him there. For I am told he is very crafty.

23 "See therefore, and take knowledge of all the lurking places where he hides; and come back to me with certainty, and I will go with you. And it shall be, if he is in the land, that I will search for him throughout all the clans of Judah."

24 So they arose and went to Ziph before Saul. But David and his men [were] in the Wilderness of Maon, in the plain on the south of Jeshimon.

25 When Saul and his men went to seek [him], they told David. Therefore he went down to the rock, and stayed in the Wilderness of Maon. And when Saul heard [that], he pursued David in the Wilderness of Maon.

26 Then Saul went on one side of the mountain, and David and his men on the other side of the mountain. So David made haste to get away from Saul, for Saul and his men were encircling David and his men to take them.

27 But a messenger came to Saul, saying, "Hasten and come, for the Philistines have invaded the land!"

28 Therefore Saul returned from pursuing David, and went against the Philistines; so they called that place the Rock of Escape.

29 Then David went up from there and dwelt in strongholds at En Gedi.

strengthened his hand in God (vv. 16, 17)—Jonathan encouraged David by reminding him of the Lord's promise to him and concern for him.

But a messenger came (v. 27)—Providentially, the Philistines were invading the land; Saul had no choice but to withdraw and postpone his pursuit of David.

En Gedi (v. 29)—an oasis on the western shore of the Dead Sea, complete with caves suitable for hiding

Understanding the Text

4) What did David do wrong when he came to Ahimelech the priest? What were the eventual results of David's choice?

_____

_____

_____

5) How did David fail to demonstrate faith when he came to Achish, king of Gath? What other options did he have?

_____

_____

_____

6) What clear evidences of God's goodness to and protection of David do you see in these three chapters?

_____

_____

_____

Cross-Reference

Consider this psalm, which many scholars believe was written during David's flight from Saul (chapter 23).

Psalm 63
1 *A Psalm of David when he was in the wilderness of Judah. O God, You [are] my God; Early will I seek You; My soul thirsts for You; My flesh longs for You In a dry and thirsty land Where there is no water.*
2 *So I have looked for You in the sanctuary, To see Your power and Your glory.*
3 *Because Your lovingkindness [is] better than life, My lips shall praise You.*
4 *Thus I will bless You while I live; I will lift up my hands in Your name.*
5 *My soul shall be satisfied as with marrow and fatness, And my mouth shall praise You with joyful lips.*

⁶ *When I remember You on my bed, I meditate on You in the [night] watches.*
⁷ *Because You have been my help, Therefore in the shadow of Your wings I will rejoice.*
⁸ *My soul follows close behind You; Your right hand upholds me.*
⁹ *But those [who] seek my life, to destroy [it], Shall go into the lower parts of the earth.*
¹⁰ *They shall fall by the sword; They shall be a portion for jackals.*
¹¹ *But the king shall rejoice in God; Everyone who swears by Him shall glory; But the mouth of those who speak lies shall be stopped.*

Exploring the Meaning

7) Psalm 63 sounds like an expression of deep faith. Yet the chapters in 1 Samuel reveal a faltering, frail David. How can these different images be reconciled?

_____

_____

_____

8) Read Psalm 52. What does David say about the treachery of Doeg the Edomite?

_____

_____

_____

9) How did Jonathan demonstrate friendship to David during this difficult time in David's life?

_____

_____

_____

Summing Up . . .

"A person's involuntary response to the unexpected is a more reliable indicator of his character than his planned reaction to a situation he anticipates. It is when we are caught off guard that our true character is most likely to show itself." —*John MacArthur*

Reflecting on the Text

10) The Scripture records David's weakness (that is, his deception due to a lack of faith). What does this indicate about the truthfulness of Scripture? Why?

_____

_____

_____

11) What specific actions can you take to insure that your responses to difficulty will be more like the trust of Psalm 63 and less like David's lying to save his skin?

_____

_____

_____

12) In a time of trial, Jonathan was an encouragement to his friend David. What friend or loved one could use your support today? What could you do to come alongside that person and spur him or her on to love and good deeds?

_____

_____

_____

Recording Your Thoughts

_____

_____

For further study, see the following passages:

Exodus 25:30	Leviticus 24:5–9	Ruth 1:4–18
1 Kings 2:26–29	Psalm 119:29	Song of Solomon 1:14
Isaiah 46:9–11	Ezekiel 16:24–25	Matthew 12:3–4
1 Thessalonians 4:4		

Lessons in Mercy

1 Samuel 24:1—26:25

Opening Thought

1) When have you been a victim of great injustice? Perhaps it was a time in which you were falsely accused. Maybe you were treated harshly by a parent, sibling, neighbor, employee, or co-worker.

_____

_____

2) What feelings did you have during this time—toward the situation, toward the person or persons mistreating you? How did you make it through?

_____

_____

Background of the Passage

The story of 1 Samuel is the story of the beginning of Israel's united kingdom. Following a long, tumultuous period of the judges, the twelve tribes asked their final judge, the prophet Samuel, for a king. Though this request grieved God, and despite stern warnings from Samuel, the people were granted a monarch named Saul.

Saul quickly proved to be unworthy to lead the people of God. He was rejected by God, who named a young shepherd boy, David, son of Jesse the Bethlehemite, as Saul's replacement. Before the transfer of power took place, however, David won the hearts of the people by killing Goliath, the Philistine giant. Seeing his kingdom slipping away, Saul became insanely jealous and even murderous. David had to flee for his life.

Chapters 24—26 find David on the run in the Judean wilderness with his band of men. Though hunted as an innocent victim, David demonstrates great mercy to his aggressor, sparing Saul's life twice.

Bible Passage

Read 24:1—26:25, noting the key words and definitions to the right of the passage.

1 Samuel 24:1—26:25

¹ Now it happened, when Saul had returned from following the Philistines, that it was told him, saying, "Take note! David [is] in the Wilderness of En Gedi."

² Then Saul took three thousand chosen men from all Israel, and went to seek David and his men on the Rocks of the Wild Goats.

³ So he came to the sheepfolds by the road, where there [was] a cave; and Saul went in to attend to his needs. (David and his men were staying in the recesses of the cave.)

⁴ Then the men of David said to him, "This is the day of which the LORD said to you, 'Behold, I will deliver your enemy into your hand, that you may do to him as it seems good to you.'" And David arose and secretly cut off a corner of Saul's robe.

⁵ Now it happened afterward that David's heart troubled him because he had cut Saul's [robe].

⁶ And he said to his men, "The LORD forbid that I should do this thing to my master, the LORD's anointed, to stretch out my hand against him, seeing he [is] the anointed of the LORD."

⁷ So David restrained his servants with [these] words, and did not allow them to rise against Saul. And Saul got up from the cave and went on [his] way.

⁸ David also arose afterward, went out of the cave, and called out to Saul, saying, "My lord the king!" And when Saul looked behind him, David stooped with his face to the earth, and bowed down.

⁹ And David said to Saul: "Why do you listen to the words of men who say, 'Indeed David seeks your harm'?

¹⁰ "Look, this day your eyes have seen that the LORD delivered you today into my hand in the cave, and

three thousand chosen men (v. 2)—the most skilled soldiers

attend to his needs (v. 3)—literally "to cover his feet," a euphemism for having a bowel movement by crouching down

this is the day (v. 4)—David's men saw this occasion as God providentially giving David a perfect opportunity to kill Saul.

David's heart troubled him (v. 5)—Since touching the king's robe was tantamount to touching the king, David felt guilty about his actions.

Lord's anointed (v. 6)—Because the Lord had put Saul into power, David saw Saul's removal from office as the Lord's prerogative.

[someone] urged [me] to kill you. But [my eye] spared you, and I said, 'I will not stretch out my hand against my lord, for he [is] the LORD's anointed.'

11 "Moreover, my father, see! Yes, see the corner of your robe in my hand! For in that I cut off the corner of your robe, and did not kill you, know and see that [there is] neither evil nor rebellion in my hand, and I have not sinned against you. Yet you hunt my life to take it.

12 "Let the LORD judge between you and me, and let the LORD avenge me on you. But my hand shall not be against you.

13 "As the proverb of the ancients says, 'Wickedness proceeds from the wicked.' But my hand shall not be against you.

14 "After whom has the king of Israel come out? Whom do you pursue? A dead dog? A flea?

15 "Therefore let the LORD be judge, and judge between you and me, and see and plead my case, and deliver me out of your hand."

16 So it was, when David had finished speaking these words to Saul, that Saul said, "[Is] this your voice, my son David?" And Saul lifted up his voice and wept.

17 Then he said to David: "You [are] more righteous than I; for you have rewarded me with good, whereas I have rewarded you with evil.

18 "And you have shown this day how you have dealt well with me; for when the LORD delivered me into your hand, you did not kill me.

19 "For if a man finds his enemy, will he let him get away safely? Therefore may the LORD reward you with good for what you have done to me this day.

20 "And now I know indeed that you shall surely be king, and that the kingdom of Israel shall be established in your hand.

21 "Therefore swear now to me by the LORD that you will not cut off my descendants after me, and that you will not destroy my name from my father's house."

22 So David swore to Saul. And Saul went home, but David and his men went up to the stronghold.

neither evil nor rebellion (v. 11)—David used the piece of robe to demonstrate to Saul that though he had been close enough to kill him, this was not his desire.

proverb (v. 13)—David's point: "I'm not the wicked man you accuse me of being, Saul."

a dead dog, a flea (v. 14)— expressions of his lowliness, harmlessness, and humility

You are more righteous than I (v. 17)—David's actions and words moved Saul, who then recognized David's right to the kingship, but still he was unwilling to relinquish it.

David swore to Saul (v. 22)— By solemn oath, David promised to preserve Saul's family and name, a pledge fulfilled through Mephibosheth (2 Samuel 9:3–13).

¹ Then Samuel died; and the Israelites gathered together and lamented for him, and buried him at his home in Ramah. And David arose and went down to the Wilderness of Paran.

² Now [there was] a man in Maon whose business [was] in Carmel, and the man [was] very rich. He had three thousand sheep and a thousand goats. And he was shearing his sheep in Carmel.

³ The name of the man [was] Nabal, and the name of his wife Abigail. And [she was] a woman of good understanding and beautiful appearance; but the man [was] harsh and evil in [his] doings. And he [was of the house of] Caleb.

⁴ When David heard in the wilderness that Nabal was shearing his sheep,

⁵ David sent ten young men; and David said to the young men, "Go up to Carmel, go to Nabal, and greet him in my name.

⁶ "And thus you shall say to him who lives [in prosperity]: 'Peace [be] to you, peace to your house, and peace to all that you have!

⁷ 'Now I have heard that you have shearers. Your shepherds were with us, and we did not hurt them, nor was there anything missing from them all the while they were in Carmel.

⁸ 'Ask your young men, and they will tell you. Therefore let [my] young men find favor in your eyes, for we come on a feast day. Please give whatever comes to your hand to your servants and to your son David.'"

⁹ So when David's young men came, they spoke to Nabal according to all these words in the name of David, and waited.

¹⁰ Then Nabal answered David's servants, and said, "Who [is] David, and who [is] the son of Jesse? There are many servants nowadays who break away each one from his master.

¹¹ "Shall I then take my bread and my water and my meat that I have killed for my shearers, and give [it] to men when I do not know where they [are] from?"

¹² So David's young men turned on their heels and went back; and they came and told him all these words.

the Israelites . . . lamented for him (25:1)—Saul's influence resulted in widespread grief at his death.

Nabal (v. 3)—The name means "fool," an appropriate name given his behavior.

Abigail (v. 3)—the wise and beautiful wife of Nabal

shearing his sheep (vv. 4–5)—David's men had protected Nabal's sheep in the wilderness (vv. 15–16), so they sought compensation for their work.

Who is David . . . ? (v. 10)—feigned ignorance as David's reputation was national; an attempt to avoid doing the right thing

13 *Then David said to his men, "Every man gird on his sword." So every man girded on his sword, and David also girded on his sword. And about four hundred men went with David, and two hundred stayed with the supplies.*

14 *Now one of the young men told Abigail, Nabal's wife, saying, "Look, David sent messengers from the wilderness to greet our master; and he reviled them.*

15 *"But the men [were] very good to us, and we were not hurt, nor did we miss anything as long as we accompanied them, when we were in the fields.*

16 *"They were a wall to us both by night and day, all the time we were with them keeping the sheep.*

17 *"Now therefore, know and consider what you will do, for harm is determined against our master and against all his household. For he [is such] a scoundrel that [one] cannot speak to him."*

18 *Then Abigail made haste and took two hundred [loaves] of bread, two skins of wine, five sheep already dressed, five seahs of roasted [grain], one hundred clusters of raisins, and two hundred cakes of figs, and loaded [them] on donkeys.*

19 *And she said to her servants, "Go on before me; see, I am coming after you." But she did not tell her husband Nabal.*

20 *So it was, as she rode on the donkey, that she went down under cover of the hill; and there were David and his men, coming down toward her, and she met them.*

21 *Now David had said, "Surely in vain I have protected all that this [fellow] has in the wilderness, so that nothing was missed of all that [belongs] to him. And he has repaid me evil for good.*

22 *"May God do so, and more also, to the enemies of David, if I leave one male of all who [belong] to him by morning light."*

23 *Now when Abigail saw David, she hastened to dismount from the donkey, fell on her face before David, and bowed down to the ground.*

24 *So she fell at his feet and said: "On me, my lord, [on] me [let] this iniquity [be]! And please let your maidservant speak in your ears, and hear the words of your maidservant.*

25 *"Please, let not my lord regard this scoundrel Nabal. For as his name [is], so [is] he: Nabal [is]*

reviled (v. 14)—Nabal viciously rebuffed David's messengers.

one cannot speak to him (v. 17)—Nabal was a worthless fellow who refused to listen to reason or wise counsel.

did not tell her husband (v. 19)—Abigail knew her husband would disapprove, but she also knew he was wrong and that harsh consequences would result from ill-treatment of the Lord's anointed.

May God do so (v. 22)—David swore to kill every male in Nabal's household by daybreak.

his name, and folly [is] with him. But I, your maid-servant, did not see the young men of my lord whom you sent.

²⁶ "Now therefore, my lord, [as] the LORD lives and [as] your soul lives, since the LORD has held you back from coming to bloodshed and from avenging yourself with your own hand, now then, let your enemies and those who seek harm for my lord be as Nabal.

²⁷ "And now this present which your maidservant has brought to my lord, let it be given to the young men who follow my lord.

²⁸ "Please forgive the trespass of your maidservant. For the LORD will certainly make for my lord an enduring house, because my lord fights the battles of the LORD, and evil is not found in you through-out your days.

²⁹ "Yet a man has risen to pursue you and seek your life, but the life of my lord shall be bound in the bundle of the living with the LORD your God; and the lives of your enemies He shall sling out, [as from] the pocket of a sling.

³⁰ "And it shall come to pass, when the LORD has done for my lord according to all the good that He has spoken concerning you, and has appointed you ruler over Israel,

³¹ "that this will be no grief to you, nor offense of heart to my lord, either that you have shed blood without cause, or that my lord has avenged himself. But when the LORD has dealt well with my lord, then remember your maidservant."

³² Then David said to Abigail: "Blessed [is] the LORD God of Israel, who sent you this day to meet me!

³³ "And blessed [is] your advice and blessed [are] you, because you have kept me this day from coming to bloodshed and from avenging myself with my own hand.

³⁴ "For indeed, [as] the LORD God of Israel lives, who has kept me back from hurting you, unless you had hastened and come to meet me, surely by morning light no males would have been left to Nabal!"

³⁵ So David received from her hand what she had brought him, and said to her, "Go up in peace to your house. See, I have heeded your voice and respected your person."

an enduring house (v. 28)— perceptive insight into the nature of the Davidic kingship/Covenant

bound in the bundle of the living (v. 29)—a metaphor that reflects the custom of binding valuables in a bundle to protect them from injury; the idea is that David enjoyed the protection of God as he was destined for great things

ruler over Israel (v. 30)— Abigail was concerned that David not endanger his future by exact-ing personal vengeance on her foolish husband.

36 *Now Abigail went to Nabal, and there he was, holding a feast in his house, like the feast of a king. And Nabal's heart [was] merry within him, for he [was] very drunk; therefore she told him nothing, little or much, until morning light.*

37 *So it was, in the morning, when the wine had gone from Nabal, and his wife had told him these things, that his heart died within him, and he became [like] a stone.*

38 *Then it came about, [after] about ten days, that the LORD struck Nabal, and he died.*

39 *So when David heard that Nabal was dead, he said, "Blessed [be] the LORD, who has pleaded the cause of my reproach from the hand of Nabal, and has kept His servant from evil! For the LORD has returned the wickedness of Nabal on his own head." And David sent and proposed to Abigail, to take her as his wife.*

40 *When the servants of David had come to Abigail at Carmel, they spoke to her saying, "David sent us to you, to ask you to become his wife."*

41 *Then she arose, bowed her face to the earth, and said, "Here is your maidservant, a servant to wash the feet of the servants of my lord."*

42 *So Abigail rose in haste and rode on a donkey, attended by five of her maidens; and she followed the messengers of David, and became his wife.*

43 *David also took Ahinoam of Jezreel, and so both of them were his wives.*

44 *But Saul had given Michal his daughter, David's wife, to Palti the son of Laish, who [was] from Gallim.*

1 *Now the Ziphites came to Saul at Gibeah, saying, "Is David not hiding in the hill of Hachilah, opposite Jeshimon?"*

2 *Then Saul arose and went down to the Wilderness of Ziph, having three thousand chosen men of Israel with him, to seek David in the Wilderness of Ziph.*

3 *And Saul encamped in the hill of Hachilah, which [is] opposite Jeshimon, by the road. But David stayed in the wilderness, and he saw that Saul came after him into the wilderness.*

4 *David therefore sent out spies, and understood that Saul had indeed come.*

heart died . . . became like a stone (vv. 37–38)—Intoxicated, Nabal apparently suffered a stroke and became paralyzed until he died.

Ahinoam of Jezreel (v. 43)—David's third wife, after Michal and Abigail

5 *So David arose and came to the place where Saul had encamped. And David saw the place where Saul lay, and Abner the son of Ner, the commander of his army. Now Saul lay within the camp, with the people encamped all around him.*

6 *Then David answered, and said to Ahimelech the Hittite and to Abishai the son of Zeruiah, brother of Joab, saying, "Who will go down with me to Saul in the camp?" And Abishai said, "I will go down with you."*

7 *So David and Abishai came to the people by night; and there Saul lay sleeping within the camp, with his spear stuck in the ground by his head. And Abner and the people lay all around him.*

8 *Then Abishai said to David, "God has delivered your enemy into your hand this day. Now therefore, please, let me strike him at once with the spear, right to the earth; and I will not [have to strike] him a second time!"*

9 *And David said to Abishai, "Do not destroy him; for who can stretch out his hand against the LORD's anointed, and be guiltless?"*

10 *David said furthermore, "[As] the LORD lives, the LORD shall strike him, or his day shall come to die, or he shall go out to battle and perish.*

11 *"The LORD forbid that I should stretch out my hand against the LORD's anointed. But please, take now the spear and the jug of water that [are] by his head, and let us go."*

12 *So David took the spear and the jug of water [by] Saul's head, and they got away; and no man saw [it] or knew [it] or awoke. For they [were] all asleep, because a deep sleep from the LORD had fallen on them.*

13 *Now David went over to the other side, and stood on the top of a hill afar off, a great distance [being] between them.*

14 *And David called out to the people and to Abner the son of Ner, saying, "Do you not answer, Abner?" Then Abner answered and said, "Who [are] you, calling out to the king?"*

15 *So David said to Abner, "[Are] you not a man? And who [is] like you in Israel? Why then have you not guarded your lord the king? For one of the people came in to destroy your lord the king.*

As the Lord lives (26:10)—a solemn oath essentially meaning that the sovereign God would (and should) decide when and where Saul would perish

spear and the jug (v. 12)— proof, as with the robe earlier, that David had been close enough to harm Saul, if that had been his desire

16 *"This thing that you have done [is] not good. [As] the LORD lives, you deserve to die, because you have not guarded your master, the LORD's anointed. And now see where the king's spear [is], and the jug of water that [was] by his head."*

17 *Then Saul knew David's voice, and said, "[Is that] your voice, my son David?" And David said, "[It is] my voice, my lord, O king."*

18 *And he said, "Why does my lord thus pursue his servant? For what have I done, or what evil [is] in my hand?*

19 *"Now therefore, please, let my lord the king hear the words of his servant: If the LORD has stirred you up against me, let Him accept an offering. But if [it is] the children of men, [may] they [be] cursed before the LORD, for they have driven me out this day from sharing in the inheritance of the LORD, saying, 'Go, serve other gods.'*

20 *"So now, do not let my blood fall to the earth before the face of the LORD. For the king of Israel has come out to seek a flea, as when one hunts a partridge in the mountains."*

21 *Then Saul said, "I have sinned. Return, my son David. For I will harm you no more, because my life was precious in your eyes this day. Indeed I have played the fool and erred exceedingly."*

22 *And David answered and said, "Here is the king's spear. Let one of the young men come over and get it.*

23 *"May the LORD repay every man [for] his righteousness and his faithfulness; for the LORD delivered you into [my] hand today, but I would not stretch out my hand against the LORD's anointed.*

24 *"And indeed, as your life was valued much this day in my eyes, so let my life be valued much in the eyes of the LORD, and let Him deliver me out of all tribulation."*

25 *Then Saul said to David, "[May] you [be] blessed, my son David! You shall both do great things and also still prevail." So David went on his way, and Saul returned to his place.*

If the Lord . . . the children of men (v. 19)—David presented two options for why Saul might be pursuing him: (1) David was in sin; if so, he was willing to offer a sacrifice for atonement; (2) Saul was listening to evil men; if so, those men should be judged.

I have sinned (v. 21)—a confession of wrongdoing, but not convincing enough apparently to cause David to return with Saul

Understanding the Text

3) What was the sequence of events the first time David spared Saul's life? Why didn't this act convince Saul of David's sincerity?

_____

_____

_____

4) In what ways did Abigail demonstrate mercy to Nabal? To David?

_____

_____

5) The second time David showed mercy to Saul, what reason(s) did he give for not hurting his adversary?

_____

_____

Cross-Reference

This psalm was likely written during the time of the events described in chapters 23—25. Note the rich background details it provides.

Psalm 142
1 *A Contemplation of David. A Prayer when he was in the cave. I cry out to the* LORD *with my voice; With my voice to the* LORD *I make my supplication.*
2 *I pour out my complaint before Him; I declare before Him my trouble.*
3 *When my spirit was overwhelmed within me, Then You knew my path. In the way in which I walk They have secretly set a snare for me.*
4 *Look on [my] right hand and see, For [there is] no one who acknowledges me; Refuge has failed me; No one cares for my soul.*
5 *I cried out to You, O* LORD: *I said, "You [are] my refuge, My portion in the land of the living.*
6 *Attend to my cry, For I am brought very low; Deliver me from my persecutors, For they are stronger than I.*
7 *Bring my soul out of prison, That I may praise Your name; The righteous shall surround me, For You shall deal bountifully with me."*

Exploring the Meaning

6) What five words would you use to describe David's emotional and spiritual state during this time of persecution by Saul?

_____

_____

7) Why do you suppose a wise and sweet woman like Abigail ever married a worthless fool like Nabal?

_____

_____

8) What do Saul's reactions to David's repeated acts of mercy and kindness reveal to you about the heart of someone who is not right with God?

_____

_____

Summing Up . . .

"In 1567 King Philip II of Spain appointed the Duke of Alba as governor of the lower part of the nation. The Duke was a bitter enemy of the newly-emerging Protestant Reformation. His rule was called the reign of terror, and his council was called the Bloody Council because it had ordered the slaughter of so many Protestants. It is reported that one man who was sentenced to die for his biblical faith managed to escape during the dead of winter. As he was being pursued by a lone soldier, the man came to a lake whose ice was thin and cracking. Somehow he managed to get safely across the ice, but as soon as he reached the other side he heard his pursuer screaming. The soldier had fallen through the ice and was about to drown. At the risk of being captured, tortured, and eventually killed—or of being drowned himself—the man went back across the lake and rescued his enemy because the love of Christ constrained him to do it. He knew he had no other choice if he was to be faithful to His Lord (Elon Foster, _New Cyclopedia of Prose Illustrations: Second Series_ [New York: T. Y. Crowell, 1877], p. 296)." —_John MacArthur_

Reflecting on the Text

9) What principles can you draw for your life from the example of David in these chapters?

_____

_____

10) What principles can you draw for your life from the example of Abigail?

_____

_____

_____

(verses to consider: Proverbs 31:10–31)

11) Based on what you've learned, write a short definition of mercy in the space below:

_____

_____

Recording Your Thoughts

_____

_____

_____

_____

For further study, see the following passages:

Genesis 2:21	Joshua 14:13	Joshua 15:13
Judges 11:27	2 Samuel 7:11–16	2 Samuel 21:7
Job 39:1	Psalm 57	Matthew 7:16, 20
Acts 5:29		

David's Defection

Opening Thought

1) Think back over your life and some of the more memorable sinful decisions you've made. In retrospect which of the following had the most influence in your choice to disobey God:

	Not a factor							A major factor		
Bad advice/counsel	(1)	2	3	4	5	6	7	8	9	10
Peer pressure	1	2	3	4	5	6	7	(8)	9	10
Powerful internal urges	1	2	3	4	5	6	(7)	8	9	10
Ignorance of God's Word	1	2	3	4	5	6	(7)	8	9	10
Frustration at waiting	(1)	2	3	4	5	6	7	8	9	10
Fear	1	2	3	(4)	5	6	7	8	9	10
Uncontrolled anger	(1)	2	3	4	5	6	7	8	9	10
Curiosity	1	2	3	(4)	5	6	7	8	9	10
Pride	1	2	3	4	5	6	(7)	8	9	10
Other: _____	1	2	3	4	5	6	7	8	9	10

Why do we need to be on our guard in desperate times? Why do we need to be on our guard in easy times? In which situations are we more likely to sin?

Desperate → short-cut, easiest path
Easy → complacent, do what's natural

Background of the Passage

On the run from Saul, David faced a bittersweet existence. He experienced some blessing (Jonathan's friendship, the kindness of Abigail, the support of some six hundred men, the protection of God). But he also felt confusion and uncertainty. If he were the Lord's anointed, then why was he being hotly pursued—especially when he had done nothing wrong?

David's occasional feelings of abandonment led to occasional expressions of deep trust (Psalms 63 and 142), but here in chapter 27, they lead to a lapse of faith.

Bible Passage

Read 27:1—28:2, noting the key words and definitions to the right of the passage

1 Samuel 27:1—28:2

1 And David said in his heart, "Now I shall perish someday by the hand of Saul. [There is] nothing better for me than that I should speedily escape to the land of the Philistines; and Saul will despair of me, to seek me anymore in any part of Israel. So I shall escape out of his hand."

2 Then David arose and went over with the six hundred men who [were] with him to Achish the son of Maoch, king of Gath.

3 So David dwelt with Achish at Gath, he and his men, each man with his household, [and] David with his two wives, Ahinoam the Jezreelitess, and Abigail the Carmelitess, Nabal's widow.

4 And it was told Saul that David had fled to Gath; so he sought him no more.

5 Then David said to Achish, "If I have now found favor in your eyes, let them give me a place in some town in the country, that I may dwell there. For why should your servant dwell in the royal city with you?"

6 So Achish gave him Ziklag that day. Therefore

by the hand of Saul (v. 1)—In contrast to both the promise of God and the word of Saul, David feared death at the hand of the king.

two wives (v. 3)—Michal, David's wife, had been given to another man by Saul.

sought him no more (v. 4)—Saul ended his pursuit when David departed from Israel.

the royal city (v. 5)—Gath; David requested a city of his own so that he might be safe from the Philistines who distrusted him and so that he might avoid their pagan influence

Ziklag (v. 6)—a city about thirteen miles northwest of Beersheeba, near the Judah/Philistine border, formerly under Israelite control but now the possession of the Philistines

Ziklag has belonged to the kings of Judah to this day.

7 *Now the time that David dwelt in the country of the Philistines was one full year and four months.*

8 *And David and his men went up and raided the Geshurites, the Girzites, and the Amalekites. For those nations were the inhabitants of the land from of old, as you go to Shur, even as far as the land of Egypt.*

9 *Whenever David attacked the land, he left neither man nor woman alive, but took away the sheep, the oxen, the donkeys, the camels, and the apparel, and returned and came to Achish.*

10 *Then Achish would say, "Where have you made a raid today?" And David would say, "Against the southern [area] of Judah, or against the southern [area] of the Jerahmeelites, or against the southern [area] of the Kenites."*

11 *David would save neither man nor woman alive, to bring [news] to Gath, saying, "Lest they should inform on us, saying, 'Thus David did.'" And thus [was] his behavior all the time he dwelt in the country of the Philistines.*

12 *So Achish believed David, saying, "He has made his people Israel utterly abhor him; therefore he will be my servant forever."*

1 *Now it happened in those days that the Philistines gathered their armies together for war, to fight with Israel. And Achish said to David, "You assuredly know that you will go out with me to battle, you and your men."*

2 *And David said to Achish, "Surely you know what your servant can do." And Achish said to David, "Therefore I will make you one of my chief guardians forever."*

one full year and four months (v. 7)—David was able to deceive Achish for sixteen months; he moved to Hebron following the death of Saul.

Geshurites . . . Girzites . . . Amalekites (v. 8)—peoples who lived in southern Canaan and northern Sinai

he left neither man nor woman alive (v. 9)—so that Achish might not learn the true nature of David's raids

Judah . . . Jerahmeelites . . . Kenites (v. 10)—David's unbelief produced the evil fruit of deception; he implied to Achish that he was attacking his own people, and that they, as a result, were increasingly hostile to him; just the opposite was true.

Understanding the Text

2) Despite God's instruction to David to stay in the land of Judah (22:5), he left for Philistine territory. Why?

Lost faith, desperate, fear of Saul

3) Why didn't David stay in the city of Gath with Achish?

note on v. 5

4) What were David's activities while living in Ziklag?

raided, looted, murdered, lied

Cross-Reference

Though the situation that prompted David to write this psalm is not known, consider how such an attitude of trust might have kept David from the wrong choices he made as recorded in chapter 27.

Psalm 31

1 *To the Chief Musician. A Psalm of David. In You, O LORD, I put my trust; Let me never be ashamed; Deliver me in Your righteousness.*

2 *Bow down Your ear to me, Deliver me speedily; Be my rock of refuge, A fortress of defense to save me.*

3 *For You [are] my rock and my fortress; Therefore, for Your name's sake, Lead me and guide me.*

4 *Pull me out of the net which they have secretly laid for me, For You [are] my strength.*

5 *Into Your hand I commit my spirit; You have redeemed me, O LORD God of truth.*

6 *I have hated those who regard useless idols; But I trust in the LORD.*

7 *I will be glad and rejoice in Your mercy, For You have considered my trouble; You have known my soul in adversities,*

8 *And have not shut me up into the hand of the enemy; You have set my feet in a wide place.*

9 *Have mercy on me, O LORD, for I am in trouble; My eye wastes away with grief, [Yes], my soul and my body!*

10 *For my life is spent with grief, And my years with sighing; My strength fails because of my iniquity, And my bones waste away.*

11 *I am a reproach among all my enemies, But especially among my neighbors, And [am] repulsive to my acquaintances; Those who see me outside flee from me.*

12 *I am forgotten like a dead man, out of mind; I am like a broken vessel.*

13 *For I hear the slander of many; Fear [is] on every side; While they take counsel together against me, They scheme to take away my life.*

14 *But as for me, I trust in You, O LORD; I say, "You [are] my God."*

15 *My times [are] in Your hand; Deliver me from the hand of my enemies, And from those who persecute me.*

16 *Make Your face shine upon Your servant; Save me for Your mercies' sake.*

17 *Do not let me be ashamed, O LORD, for I have called upon You; Let the wicked be ashamed; Let them be silent in the grave.*

18 *Let the lying lips be put to silence, Which speak insolent things proudly and contemptuously against the righteous.*

19 *Oh, how great [is] Your goodness, Which You have laid up for those who fear You, [Which] You have prepared for those who trust in You In the presence of the sons of men!*

20 *You shall hide them in the secret place of Your presence From the plots of man; You shall keep them secretly in a pavilion From the strife of tongues.*

21 *Blessed [be] the LORD, For He has shown me His marvelous kindness in a strong city!*

²² *For I said in my haste, "I am cut off from before Your eyes"; Nevertheless You heard the voice of my supplications When I cried out to You.*

²³ *Oh, love the LORD, all you His saints! [For] the LORD preserves the faithful, And fully repays the proud person.*

²⁴ *Be of good courage, And He shall strengthen your heart, All you who hope in the LORD.*

Exploring the Meaning

5) How are David's actions in chapter 27 at odds with his words in Psalm 31?

Did not trust or follow God's plan

6) We know that God is in control of our lives, but we also know that He expects us to do certain things. The life of faith is not a life of inaction.

What were David's other options rather than fleeing to the Philistines? What should he have done?

Prayed, sought aid from allies – other people of God, followed God's command

7) Read 1 Corinthians 10:13. How does the truth of this verse apply to David's difficult situation? How can a person know whether a particular choice is a God-given "way of escape"?

Summing Up . . .

"Worry is the sin of distrusting the promise and providence of God, and yet it is a sin that Christians commit perhaps more frequently than any other. The English term *worry* comes from an old German word meaning to strangle or choke. That is exactly what worry does; it is a kind of mental and emotional strangulation, which probably causes more mental and physical affliction than any other single cause.

"It has been reported that a dense fog extensive enough to cover seven city blocks a hundred feet deep is composed of less than one glass of water—divided into sixty thousand million droplets. In the right form, a few gallons of water can cripple a large city.

"In a similar way, the substance of worry is nearly always extremely small compared to the size it forms in our minds and the damage it does in our lives. Someone has said, 'Worry is a thin stream of fear that trickles through the mind, which, if encouraged, will cut a channel so wide that all other thoughts will be drained out." —*John MacArthur*

Reflecting on the Text

8) How often does worry (losing sight of the promise and providence of God) create a sense of panic in you that results in your making wrong choices?

Unsure

9) An old spiritual has a chorus that says, "God may make you wait, but He'll never be too late." In what area of life, in what situation, are you fretting (and considering a rash, and possibly sinful decision) because God is asking you to wait for *Him* to work?

Family's salvation?

10) How would you have advised David if he had come to you with his idea about moving in with the Philistines? Why?

_____

_____

_____

_____

Recording Your Thoughts

_____

_____

_____

_____

_____

_____

_____

_____

_____

_____

_____

_____

For further study, see the following passages:

Joshua 15:31	Joshua 19:5	1 Samuel 25:44
1 Samuel 26:25	2 Samuel 1:1	Psalm 56

A Sad End to a Sorry Life

Opening Thought

1) If your life were ending tomorrow, of what would you be most proud? Why?

_____

_____

2) Who is someone you admire for living an extraordinary life? What makes that person's life so amazing?

Judge Osteen _____

_____

What makes for a full, meaningful, and fruitful life?

_____

_____

3) What action or actions would cause you to view your life as a total disgrace? Why?

Nothing _____

_____

Background of the Passage

With Samuel dead and David still in hiding, Saul feels spiritually and militarily vulnerable. His fear and paranoia reach a fever pitch when the Philistine army makes a powerful and threatening push into Israelite territory.

So desperate is Saul for counsel that he commits the heinous sin of consulting a spiritistic medium in an attempt to conjure up the spirit of Samuel. God—much to the medium's shock and to Saul's horror—actually allows the deceased prophet to speak words of rebuke to the wicked king.

Meanwhile David, despite an apparent willingness to fight against his own people, has been dismissed by the suspicious warlords of the Philistines, over the objections of King Achish.

Then, perhaps due to his own faithlessness, David experiences a measure of chastening at the hands of Amalekite raiders who steal the livestock and kidnap the wives of David and his fighting men. In the end, however, because of God's graciousness, David and his band prevail, conquering the Amalekites and rescuing their loved ones.

Saul is not so fortunate. As prophesied, he and his sons are slain in battle with the Philistines. The king who began his reign with such promise ends in terrible disgrace.

Bible Passage

Read 28:3—31:13, noting the key words and definitions to the right of the passage.

1 Samuel 28:3—31:13

3 Now Samuel had died, and all Israel had lamented for him and buried him in Ramah, in his own city. And Saul had put the mediums and the spiritists out of the land.

4 Then the Philistines gathered together, and came and encamped at Shunem. So Saul gathered all Israel together, and they encamped at Gilboa.

5 When Saul saw the army of the Philistines, he was afraid, and his heart trembled greatly.

6 And when Saul inquired of the LORD, the LORD did not answer him, either by dreams or by Urim or by the prophets.

7 Then Saul said to his servants, "Find me a woman who is a medium, that I may go to her and inquire of her." And his servants said to him, "In fact, [there is] a woman who is a medium at En Dor."

8 So Saul disguised himself and put on other clothes, and he went, and two men with him; and they came to the woman by night. And he said, "Please conduct

mediums and spiritists (v. 3)—Despite a divine ban of occult activities, and though Saul had previously implemented this rule strictly, he turned to a medium in his foolish attempt to find some measure of guidance.

his heart trembled greatly (v. 5)—Saul was deathly afraid because of the loss of the Spirit and his own decline into sin.

dreams . . . Urim . . . prophets (v. 6)—Saul's disobedience effectively cut him off from the three primary ways that God would communicate with his people in Old Testament times.

a seance for me, and bring up for me the one I shall name to you."

9 Then the woman said to him, "Look, you know what Saul has done, how he has cut off the mediums and the spiritists from the land. Why then do you lay a snare for my life, to cause me to die?"

10 And Saul swore to her by the LORD, saying, "[As] the LORD lives, no punishment shall come upon you for this thing."

11 Then the woman said, "Whom shall I bring up for you?" And he said, "Bring up Samuel for me."

12 When the woman saw Samuel, she cried out with a loud voice. And the woman spoke to Saul, saying, "Why have you deceived me? For you [are] Saul!"

13 And the king said to her, "Do not be afraid. What did you see?" And the woman said to Saul, "I saw a spirit ascending out of the earth."

14 So he said to her, "What [is] his form?" And she said, "An old man is coming up, and he [is] covered with a mantle." And Saul perceived that it [was] Samuel, and he stooped with [his] face to the ground and bowed down.

15 Now Samuel said to Saul, "Why have you disturbed me by bringing me up?" And Saul answered, "I am deeply distressed; for the Philistines make war against me, and God has departed from me and does not answer me anymore, neither by prophets nor by dreams. Therefore I have called you, that you may reveal to me what I should do."

16 Then Samuel said: "Why then do you ask me, seeing the LORD has departed from you and has become your enemy?

17 "And the LORD has done for Himself as He spoke by me. For the LORD has torn the kingdom out of your hand and given it to your neighbor, David.

18 "Because you did not obey the voice of the LORD nor execute His fierce wrath upon Amalek, therefore the LORD has done this thing to you this day.

19 "Moreover the LORD will also deliver Israel with you into the hand of the Philistines. And tomorrow you and your sons [will be] with me. The LORD will also deliver the army of Israel into the hand of the Philistines."

20 Then immediately Saul fell full length on the ground, and was dreadfully afraid because of the words of Samuel. And there was no strength in him, for he had eaten no food all day or all night.

21 And the woman came to Saul and saw that he was severely troubled, and said to him, "Look, your maid-servant has obeyed your voice, and I have put my life in my hands and heeded the words which you spoke to me.

So Saul disguised himself (v. 8)—Saul's actions, taken at night, reveal his guilt.

swore to her by the Lord (v. 10)—How ironic that Saul took an oath in the name of the Lord he was disobeying to get a banned medium to give him forbidden guidance.

the woman saw Samuel (v. 12)—This was not an apparition but an actual appearance by the spirit of Samuel; the medium's shock indicates this was totally unexpected and suggests that God miraculously arranged this supernatural event to show his power to the medium and to reveal Saul.

old man . . . with a mantle (v. 14)—Though old age and clothing do not exist in the spiritual realm, these characteristics enabled Saul to perceive that the spirit was Samuel's.

disturbed me (v. 15)—Samuel was agitated with Saul's blatant disregard for the law in consulting the dead through a medium.

will be with me (v. 19)—a premonition of the impending deaths of Saul and his sons

no strength in him (v. 20)—Saul was completely weakened and disheartened due to shock and fear; he returned to his camp to await his doom.

22 *"Now therefore, please, heed also the voice of your maidservant, and let me set a piece of bread before you; and eat, that you may have strength when you go on [your] way."*

23 *But he refused and said, "I will not eat." So his servants, together with the woman, urged him; and he heeded their voice. Then he arose from the ground and sat on the bed.*

24 *Now the woman had a fatted calf in the house, and she hastened to kill it. And she took flour and kneaded [it], and baked unleavened bread from it.*

25 *So she brought [it] before Saul and his servants, and they ate. Then they rose and went away that night.*

1 *Then the Philistines gathered together all their armies at Aphek, and the Israelites encamped by a fountain which [is] in Jezreel.*

2 *And the lords of the Philistines passed in review by hundreds and by thousands, but David and his men passed in review at the rear with Achish.*

3 *Then the princes of the Philistines said, "What [are] these Hebrews [doing here]?" And Achish said to the princes of the Philistines, "[Is] this not David, the servant of Saul king of Israel, who has been with me these days, or these years? And to this day I have found no fault in him since he defected [to me]."*

4 *But the princes of the Philistines were angry with him; so the princes of the Philistines said to him, "Make this fellow return, that he may go back to the place which you have appointed for him, and do not let him go down with us to battle, lest in the battle he become our adversary. For with what could he reconcile himself to his master, if not with the heads of these men?*

5 *"[Is] this not David, of whom they sang to one another in dances, saying: 'Saul has slain his thousands, And David his ten thousands'?"*

6 *Then Achish called David and said to him, "Surely, [as] the LORD lives, you have been upright, and your going out and your coming in with me in the army [is] good in my sight. For to this day I have not found evil in you since the day of your coming to me. Nevertheless the lords do not favor you.*

7 *"Therefore return now, and go in peace, that you may not displease the lords of the Philistines."*

8 *So David said to Achish, "But what have I done? And to this day what have you found in your servant as long as I have been with you, that I may not go and fight against the enemies of my lord the king?"*

9 *Then Achish answered and said to David, "I know that you [are] as good in my sight as an angel of God; nevertheless the princes of the Philistines have said, 'He shall not go up with us to the battle.'*

10 *"Now therefore, rise early in the morning with your*

gathered . . . encamped
(29:1)—a return to the story-line interrupted in 28:1 by Saul's visit to the medium

he became our adversary
(v. 4)—The Philistine lords were suspicious of David, thinking that his friendship was likely feigned and that in battle he would double-cross Achish.

David, of whom they sang
(v. 5)—David's fame had spread even to Philistia.

the enemies of my lord and king (v. 8)—David may have been pretending to be loyal to Achish or this may have been another lapse in faith in judgment and a real promise to take up arms against his Israelite brothers.

master's servants who have come with you. And as soon as you are up early in the morning and have light, depart."

11 So David and his men rose early to depart in the morning, to return to the land of the Philistines. And the Philistines went up to Jezreel.

1 Now it happened, when David and his men came to Ziklag, on the third day, that the Amalekites had invaded the South and Ziklag, attacked Ziklag and burned it with fire,

2 and had taken captive the women and those who [were] there, from small to great; they did not kill anyone, but carried [them] away and went their way.

3 So David and his men came to the city, and there it was, burned with fire; and their wives, their sons, and their daughters had been taken captive.

4 Then David and the people who [were] with him lifted up their voices and wept, until they had no more power to weep.

5 And David's two wives, Ahinoam the Jezreelitess, and Abigail the widow of Nabal the Carmelite, had been taken captive.

6 Now David was greatly distressed, for the people spoke of stoning him, because the soul of all the people was grieved, every man for his sons and his daughters. But David strengthened himself in the LORD his God.

7 Then David said to Abiathar the priest, Ahimelech's son, "Please bring the ephod here to me." And Abiathar brought the ephod to David.

8 So David inquired of the LORD, saying, "Shall I pursue this troop? Shall I overtake them?" And He answered him, "Pursue, for you shall surely overtake [them] and without fail recover [all]."

9 So David went, he and the six hundred men who [were] with him, and came to the Brook Besor, where those stayed who were left behind.

10 But David pursued, he and four hundred men; for two hundred stayed [behind], who were so weary that they could not cross the Brook Besor.

11 Then they found an Egyptian in the field, and brought him to David; and they gave him bread and he ate, and they let him drink water.

12 And they gave him a piece of a cake of figs and two clusters of raisins. So when he had eaten, his strength came back to him; for he had eaten no bread nor drunk water for three days and three nights.

13 Then David said to him, "To whom do you [belong], and where [are] you from?" And he said, "I [am] a young man from Egypt, servant of an Amalekite; and my master left me behind, because three days ago I fell sick.

14 "We made an invasion of the southern [area] of the

Amalekites (30:1)—Reaping the consequences of Saul's failure to wipe out the Amalekites, David and his men found themselves the victims of a raid in which their wives and livestock were captured.

strengthened himself in the Lord his God (v. 6)—David found renewed hope and courage through his deep faith and close walk with God (as evidenced in the Psalms).

Abiathar brought the ephod (v. 7)—David was desperate to know God's will.

Cherethites, in the [territory] which [belongs] to Judah, and of the southern [area] of Caleb; and we burned Ziklag with fire."

¹⁵ *And David said to him, "Can you take me down to this troop?" So he said, "Swear to me by God that you will neither kill me nor deliver me into the hands of my master, and I will take you down to this troop."*

¹⁶ *And when he had brought him down, there they were, spread out over all the land, eating and drinking and dancing, because of all the great spoil which they had taken from the land of the Philistines and from the land of Judah.*

¹⁷ *Then David attacked them from twilight until the evening of the next day. Not a man of them escaped, except four hundred young men who rode on camels and fled.*

¹⁸ *So David recovered all that the Amalekites had carried away, and David rescued his two wives.*

¹⁹ *And nothing of theirs was lacking, either small or great, sons or daughters, spoil or anything which they had taken from them; David recovered all.*

²⁰ *Then David took all the flocks and herds they had driven before those [other] livestock, and said, "This [is] David's spoil."*

²¹ *Now David came to the two hundred men who had been so weary that they could not follow David, whom they also had made to stay at the Brook Besor. So they went out to meet David and to meet the people who [were] with him. And when David came near the people, he greeted them.*

²² *Then all the wicked and worthless men of those who went with David answered and said, "Because they did not go with us, we will not give them [any] of the spoil that we have recovered, except for every man's wife and children, that they may lead [them] away and depart."*

²³ *But David said, "My brethren, you shall not do so with what the LORD has given us, who has preserved us and delivered into our hand the troop that came against us.*

²⁴ *"For who will heed you in this matter? But as his part [is] who goes down to the battle, so [shall] his part [be] who stays by the supplies; they shall share alike."*

²⁵ *So it was, from that day forward; he made it a statute and an ordinance for Israel to this day.*

²⁶ *Now when David came to Ziklag, he sent [some] of the spoil to the elders of Judah, to his friends, saying, "Here is a present for you from the spoil of the enemies of the LORD"—*

²⁷ *to [those] who [were] in Bethel, [those] who [were] in Ramoth of the South, [those] who [were] in Jattir,*

²⁸ *[those] who [were] in Aroer, [those] who [were] in Siphmoth, [those] who [were] in Eshtemoa,*

all the great spoil (v. 16)—not only their own belongings, but the plunder from all their raids, which David shared freely

nothing . . . was lacking (v. 19)—Despite David's failures, God proved to be entirely gracious.

wicked and worthless men (v. 22)—Though they were skilled fighters, the men who gathered to David during his years of exile were malcontents and of questionable character.

a statute and an ordinance (v. 25)—Over the objections of many, David legislated a practice of kindness and equity.

29 *[those] who [were] in Rachal, [those] who [were] in the cities of the Jerahmeelites, [those] who [were] in the cities of the Kenites,*

30 *[those] who [were] in Hormah, [those] who [were] in Chorashan, [those] who [were] in Athach,*

31 *[those] who [were] in Hebron, and to all the places where David himself and his men were accustomed to rove.*

1 *Now the Philistines fought against Israel; and the men of Israel fled from before the Philistines, and fell slain on Mount Gilboa.*

2 *Then the Philistines followed hard after Saul and his sons. And the Philistines killed Jonathan, Abinadab, and Malchishua, Saul's sons.*

3 *The battle became fierce against Saul. The archers hit him, and he was severely wounded by the archers.*

4 *Then Saul said to his armorbearer, "Draw your sword, and thrust me through with it, lest these uncircumcised men come and thrust me through and abuse me." But his armorbearer would not, for he was greatly afraid. Therefore Saul took a sword and fell on it.*

5 *And when his armorbearer saw that Saul was dead, he also fell on his sword, and died with him.*

6 *So Saul, his three sons, his armorbearer, and all his men died together that same day.*

7 *And when the men of Israel who [were] on the other side of the valley, and [those] who [were] on the other side of the Jordan, saw that the men of Israel had fled and that Saul and his sons were dead, they forsook the cities and fled; and the Philistines came and dwelt in them.*

8 *So it happened the next day, when the Philistines came to strip the slain, that they found Saul and his three sons fallen on Mount Gilboa.*

9 *And they cut off his head and stripped off his armor, and sent [word] throughout the land of the Philistines, to proclaim [it in] the temple of their idols and among the people.*

10 *Then they put his armor in the temple of the Ashtoreths, and they fastened his body to the wall of Beth Shan.*

11 *Now when the inhabitants of Jabesh Gilead heard what the Philistines had done to Saul,*

12 *all the valiant men arose and traveled all night, and took the body of Saul and the bodies of his sons from the wall of Beth Shan; and they came to Jabesh and burned them there.*

13 *Then they took their bones and buried [them] under the tamarisk tree at Jabesh, and fasted seven days.*

uncircumcised men (v. 4)— a term of derision among Israelites

abuse (v. 4)—Conquered kings could expect vicious and barbaric treatment.

Saul took a sword and fell on it (v. 4)—Saul ended his own sad life by suicide, the ultimate expression of faithlessness towards God.

all his men (v. 6)—all who were personally assigned to his special guard; some, like Abner (see 2 Samuel 2:8) survived

cut off his head (v. 9)—probably done as revenge for the defeat and beheading of Goliath by David

the Ashtoreths (v. 10)—fertility goddesses worshipped by the Philistines

bones . . . buried (v. 13)— It was considered disrespectful not to bury the dead.

fasted seven days (v. 13)— a sign of respect and mourning in Hebrew culture

Understanding the Text

4) In Saul's encounter with the medium, what happened to surprise Saul and the woman?

_____

_____

5) Why did the Philistines turn against David? What events caused David's own men to speak of stoning him?

_____

_____

6) What controversy broke out among David's men following the defeat of the Amalekites? How was it resolved?

_____

_____

Cross-Reference

Second Samuel 1:17–27 reveals David's grief upon learning of the death of Saul and Jonathan.

[17] *Then David lamented with this lamentation over Saul and over Jonathan his son,*
[18] *and he told [them] to teach the children of Judah [the Song of] the Bow; indeed [it is] written in the Book of Jasher:*
[19] *"The beauty of Israel is slain on your high places! How the mighty have fallen!*
[20] *Tell [it] not in Gath, Proclaim [it] not in the streets of Ashkelon—Lest the daughters of the Philistines rejoice, Lest the daughters of the uncircumcised triumph.*
[21] *"O mountains of Gilboa, [Let there be] no dew nor rain upon you, Nor fields of offerings. For the shield of the mighty is cast away there! The shield of Saul, not anointed with oil.*
[22] *From the blood of the slain, From the fat of the mighty, The bow of Jonathan did not turn back, And the sword of Saul did not return empty.*
[23] *"Saul and Jonathan [were] beloved and pleasant in their lives, And in their death they were not divided; They were swifter than eagles, They were stronger than lions.*
[24] *"O daughters of Israel, weep over Saul, Who clothed you in scarlet, with luxury; Who put ornaments of gold on your apparel.*
[25] *"How the mighty have fallen in the midst of the battle! Jonathan [was] slain in your high places.*

²⁶ *I am distressed for you, my brother Jonathan; You have been very pleasant to me;*
Your love to me was wonderful, Surpassing the love of women.
²⁷ *"How the mighty have fallen, And the weapons of war perished!"*

Exploring the Meaning

7) It is not difficult to understand why David mourned the death of Jonathan, his covenant friend. But why was David so grief-stricken over the death of Saul?

_____

_____

8) Read Leviticus 20:6, 27. What were the requirements of the Old Testament law for dealing with mediums and spiritists?

_____

_____

9) In a very dark time, the writer records that David "strengthened himself in the Lord his God" (30:6). What does this mean? How does this strengthening come about?

_____

_____

_____

Summing Up . . .

"A person who does not avoid every sin and is not meticulously obedient cannot be guarded against great sins. The sin in which he lives will always be an inlet, an open door, by which Satan will find entrance. It is like a breach in your fortress through which the enemy may get in and find his way to hurt you greatly. If you have fallen into some horrible sin, perhaps this is the reason.

"Or if you allow some way of sin as an outlet for your own corruption, it will be like a breach in a dam, which if left alone will grow bigger and bigger until it cannot be stopped." *—John MacArthur*

Reflecting on the Text

10) As you ponder both the sad life of Saul and the statement above, are you aware of any unconfessed sin in your life, any areas which are not yielded to the Lordship of Christ? Can you think of a time where one "little" sin lead to "bigger" sins in your life? What happened?

_____

_____

11) What lesson(s) do you see in David's response to the near mutiny by his men? How can this help you the next time you are discouraged or facing a big trial?

_____

_____

12) How would you summarize Saul's life? What admirable quality of his would you want to emulate? What flaws or sinful choices of his will you prayerfully avoid this week?

_____

_____

Recording Your Thoughts

_____

_____

_____

For further study, see the following passages:

Genesis 23:4–15	Exodus 17:8–16	Exodus 28:30
Leviticus 19:31	Numbers 12:6	Numbers 13:6, 30
Deuteronomy 18:11	1 Samuel 15	2 Samuel 5:17–25
Esther 3:1, 10–13	Amos 7:12–13	Acts 13:22